# COLLEGE TEACHING:
# A SYSTEMATIC APPROACH

# COLLEGE TEACHING:
# A SYSTEMATIC APPROACH

SECOND EDITION

**JAMES W. BROWN**
*Dean, Graduate Studies and Research*
*San Jose State College*

**JAMES W. THORNTON, JR.**
*Provost, Honolulu Community College*

McGRAW-HILL BOOK COMPANY

*New York, St. Louis, San Francisco, Düsseldorf, Johannesburg, Kuala Lumpur, London, Mexico, Montreal, New Delhi, Panama, Rio de Janeiro, Singapore, Sydney, Toronto*

**College Teaching: A Systematic Approach**

Library of Congress Catalog Card Number 76-127967
07-008481-5
 234567890MAMM798765432 ̣

*This book was set in Press Roman by Visual Skills, Inc., and
printed on permanent paper and bound by The Maple Press Company.
The designer was Visual Skills, Inc. The editor was William
Willey. Loretta Palma supervised production.*

# preface

The quality of teaching in college attracted more attention during the decade of the sixties than ever before in the history of American higher education. Observers from every walk of life formed opinions about it and expressed them freely. Politicians, parents, students, news commentators, alumni, dropouts, and men and women on the street were quick to criticize. College shortcomings were said to include, among many others, high costs, lack of purpose, overemphasis on vocationalism, impracticality, the admission of too many students, and the exclusion of too many students. The students themselves eagerly adopted the sport, in many instances violently, shouting the battlecry of "irrelevance."

Professors themselves suspected that there might be a good deal of merit in the charges. Partly as a result of the hue and cry, more than a dozen major centers for the study of higher education were established at universities during the decade, and began to conduct research and to publish monographs on all aspects of higher education. An indication of the interest in the "knowledge industry" is found in the 1969 edition of a very useful annual bibliography of higher education.[1] Although Kelsey notes that not all publishers submit titles and the list is not inclusive, the Bibliography lists 1,315 publications, almost all

[1] Roger R. Kelsey, compiler. *AAHE Bibliography on Higher Education,* 1969 edition. Available annually at Conference of the American Association for Higher Education, or for $1.00 from Mr. Kelsey at 700 Ludlow Street, Takoma Park, Md. 20012.

issued since 1960. Major sections of the bibliography are on college faculty, college students, college purposes, and college teaching. The scope of the concern about the quality of effective learning in college justifies the revision and modernization of our 1963 volume on *College Teaching*.

The earlier edition has been thoroughly revised to reflect the research that has been published since 1963, and also to recognize the growing importance of the systems approach in higher education. The first two chapters concentrate on the human element in higher education, the student and the professor. Chapter Three applies the concepts of systems analysis to the instructional process. The remaining three chapters deal in turn with varieties of instructional modes, nonhuman resources for instruction, and evaluation and feedback.

The authors have kept in mind during the revision, as they did in the first edition, the needs of the beginning or prospective college teacher. The book is organized on the assumption that most readers will be persons of wide experience and competence in their subject fields, but with relatively little previous acquaintance with the broad aspects of higher education or with the specifics of classroom instruction. It will thus be of particular value to individuals who are enrolled as graduate students, who have been employed as teaching assistants, and who have enrolled concurrently in a graduate seminar on college teaching. But the book will also be of value to more experienced college instructors. It will remind them of promising classroom practices, both new and old, and encourage functional, systematic approaches to improved college teaching.

*James W. Brown*
*James W. Thornton, Jr.*

# contents

# COLLEGE TEACHING:
# A SYSTEMATIC APPROACH

# chapter one / COLLEGE STUDENTS AND COLLEGE TEACHING /

DIVERSITIES IN STUDENT POPULATIONS • COLLEGE APTI-
TUDE OF STUDENTS • THE GROWING COLLEGE POPULA-
TION • ADDITIONAL ASPECTS OF THE STUDENT BODY
• THE STUDENT AND COLLEGE PURPOSES • STANDARDS
OF STUDENT ACHIEVEMENT • SUMMARY

During the decade of the sixties the total number of college and university degree credit students more than doubled. It has become trite to point out that during this ten-year period the United States was required to provide as much new opportunity for higher education as was provided over its entire earlier history. But even more significant changes in the characteristics of students took place. Activism, student militance, search for relevance, experimental colleges, free universities, strikes, protests, and demonstrations are no longer novel in higher education, but have become more widespread and more intense during recent college generations. Today, the effective college teacher must have a clear understanding of basic facts about college students, and sympathetic insight into their quandaries, their quests, and their quixotism. Perceptions of this nature are fundamental both to decisions about the emerging and the persisting purposes of colleges and to the selection of styles and techniques of teaching in our times.

A single indication of the importance that recent research ascribes to student characteristics is the fact that *Inventory of Current Research on Higher Education, 1968,* devotes 57 of its 178 pages to summaries of studies about students, and an additional four pages to "Faculty-Student Interaction."[1] Some of the

---

[1] Dale M. Heckman and Warren Bryan Martin, *Inventory of Current Research on Higher Education, 1968* (New York: McGraw-Hill Book Company, 1969).

**Figure 1-1.**
Activism, student militance, protests, and demonstrations are no longer novel in higher education. Today, the effective college teacher must seek to understand a number of basic facts about his students: their quandaries, their quests, and their quixotism. (San Jose State College)

subtopics within the category of "Students" are college environment, effects of the college experience, values, student characteristics, attrition, teaching and learning. Another clue to the growing recognition of the importance of the student in higher education is that the preponderance of book titles in the advanced education field during the latter half of the sixties dealt with *The College and The Student,*[2] *The College Student and His Culture,*[3] *Students and Teachers,*[4] and topics similarly oriented to the learner rather than to the teacher or the institution.

[2] Lawrence E. Dennis and Joseph F. Kauffman (eds.), *The College and the Student* (Washington: American Council on Education, 1966).

[3] Kaoru Yamamoto, *The College Student and His Culture: An Analysis* (Boston: Houghton Mifflin Company, 1968).

[4] Nevitt Sanford, *Students and Teachers* (San Francisco: Jossey-Bass, Inc., 1969).

This chapter presents interpretative and factual material about the American college student and attempts to demonstrate the effect his new concern for relevance is having on his institution and on the purposes of the system of higher education in America. The intention of this chapter is to present a defensible picture of the diversity and similarities of college students without obscuring the fact that every college student deviates in some degree from statistical norms. In the classroom, each student achieves or avoids education as an individual person, not as part of a category or a statistic. The statistics can nonetheless provide a sound basis for the effective efforts of the professor; it is for that reason that they are presented here.

## DIVERSITIES IN STUDENT POPULATIONS

A useful concept for understanding student bodies in colleges of different types is that of "student subcultures," as developed by Clark and Trow.[5] The basic premise is that college students bring with them broad and overlapping kinds of backgrounds that may be reinforced by the faculty and college traditions; on the other hand, their backgrounds may be quite alien to the formal purposes of education. The disparity between the values and purposes of the students and those of the institution may lead to stress as the forces of the college culture confront the resistance of the student subcultures.

> The most widely held stereotype of college life in America pictures the 'collegiate subculture,' a world of football, fraternities and sororities, dates, cars and drinking, and campus fun. The leading symbols of this subculture are the star athlete, the homecoming queen, and the fraternity dance. A good deal of student life on many campuses revolves around this subculture; it both provides substance for the stereotypes of movies and cartoons and models itself on those stereotypes.[6]

In a college where the dominant subculture is collegiate, students and faculty follow their separate paths in a sort of friendly symbiosis—sharing the same life

---

[5] Burton R. Clark, *Educating the Expert Society* (San Francisco: Chandler Publishing Company, 1962). The discussion in this section is based on Chapter 6, "Student Culture in College."

[6] *Ibid.,* p. 203.

space, but comparatively untouched each by the other. Students attend classes as the concession that they must make to the system that justifies the real business, as they see it, of college. They earn grades that will permit them to remain, but not so high as to attract the attention of their professors or the derision of their peers. The collegiate subculture requires money and time for its support, and so has little attraction for the working and the commuting student. It flourishes most notably on large campuses outside of the central city, where significant numbers of students live on or near campus and apart from their parents.

Writing in 1962, Clark recognized the incipient decline of the collegiate subculture under the pressures of competition for college records that will impress after-college employers. He attributed this decline largely to the technological revolution, the Cold War, and large business and industrial organization. At that time, he could not have foreseen the effect of the Vietnam War, the threat of Selective Service, and the several levels of protest on the campus in attracting students away from the collegiate subculture into the 'nonconformist subculture.'

The nonconformist subculture has little respect for or concern with the college. In recent days, it has been more likely to cry "Close it up! Burn it down!" than to support student activities or any other aspect of institutional life.

> To a greater degree than the academically oriented, these students use off-campus groups and currents of thought as points of reference over against the official college . . . . The distinctive quality of this student style is a rather aggressive nonconformism, which usually includes a critical detachment from the college they attend and a general hostility to the college administration. The forms this style takes vary from campus to campus, but where it exists it has a visibility and influence far beyond its usually tiny, fluid membership. Its significance lies in offering a home, an alternative, to the rebellious student seeking a distinctive identity in keeping with his own temperament and experience; in a sense it provides some *intellectual* substance to the idealism and rebelliousness generated in adolescence in some parts of Amerian society.[7]

Salient institutional developments of the 1960s have been the growth in size

[7]*Ibid.,* p. 209.

and influence on many campuses of this nonconformist subculture, its spread into the ranks of the teaching assistants and even the tenured faculty, and the assurance and determination with which it pursues its intransigent and nonnegotiable demands. Not only in America but in all parts of the world, student unrest has become a subject for attention from academicians and from legislators, trustees, taxpayers, parents, police, and all elements of society. Students of this orientation have allied themselves to emerging minority protesters, and have attracted the support of nonacademic subcultures as well. On many campuses, the demands of this subculture and its allies have usurped the attention of administrators and many faculty members, thereby delaying solutions to those problems to which the dissidents intend to call attention. Estimates of the proportion of the student body on any campus who belong to the nonconformist subculture vary widely, from as little as two or three percent to as much as fifteen or twenty percent; but their effect on the daily routines and the curriculum is undeniably out of proportion to their numbers.

The increasing enrollment of students of lower middle class families who are

**Figure 1-2.**
Concern with today's problems—including those of the ecological environment—is reflected in the contributions of this "architect of tomorrow."

motivated by the hope of upward mobility has caused the 'vocational subculture' to become a dominant influence on the character of many campuses.

> Students who are immediately and narrowly inclined toward job preparation appear in largest numbers in state colleges and technical schools, but they also bulk large at the state universities and even in many private colleges that are publicly identified as liberal-arts colleges. Vocational motivation can be combined with the collegiate life, of course, especially for those with money. Vocationalism has its purest expression among those who pull themselves through, financially, by the skin of their teeth . . . . like the participants in the collegiate subculture they are resistant to intellectual demands beyond what is required to pass the courses. To many of these hard-driven students, ideas and scholarship are as much a luxury and distraction as are sports and fraternities.[8]

The vocational subculture has been a growing threat and a disruptive influence in higher education. As a response to the dismay of graduates who find that they have been inadequately prepared for a world that requires every man to earn his keep, liberal arts colleges have introduced elements of vocationalism into the curriculum. Economics shades into business; courses required for teaching certificates are introduced in the senior year; and the preprofessional aspects of science and mathematics are emphasized.

The vocational subculture has also been a conservative counterbalance to the demands of the nonconformists for reform. Students in engineering, business, applied sciences, and education find the pressures of employment requirements so severe that they have little inclination to protest or to be patient with interruptions caused by nonconformist students. It is possible to decry the vocationalism, the presentism, and the materialism of this production-oriented segment of the college population; but it is probable that they are the dominant subculture in most public institutions. Their needs will continue to exert compelling influence on the nature of higher education in America.

The fourth subculture identified by Clark is the one for which (in the minds of the faculty) the college exists. The 'academic subculture' includes

> the students who work hard, get the best grades, but also talk about their course work outside of class and let the world of ideas and knowledge reach them. . . . This is the climate encouraged at the academically strongest

[8] *Ibid.*, p. 207.

**Figure 1-3.**
The vocational subculture of the modern college seems likely to continue to influence the nature of much of higher education.

colleges; and, when colleges aim to upgrade themselves, it is the students already oriented in this direction whom they seek to recruit .... The distinctive qualities of this group are (a) they are seriously pursuing ideas beyond the minimum required for passing and graduation, and (b) they identify themselves with their college and its faculty.[9]

Boundaries between the subcultures do overlap. A student whose primary motivation is vocational may find himself attracted to and participating in the activities of the academic or the collegiate subculture. The nonconformist subculture may recruit support from members of the academic subculture. Probably no student is so completely absorbed in one of these divisions as to be impervious to influences from members of the other groups. One of the major objectives of the faculty might well be to stimulate students to broaden their horizons so as to gain insight into the subcultures that they scorn.

The concept of subcultures can also assist in informal classification of institutions, to better understand higher education and counsel students about choice of college. Each college has its own distinctive, undefinable climate which determines its influence on its graduates. Academic prestige or the lack of it depends on intangibles, often on the aura of a past glory. If it were possible to quantify an institution by the cultural makeup of its student body, prospective students (or professors) could judge whether or not they would find stimulation and satisfaction there or, conversely, be part of a minority frustrated by countervailing majority cultures.

## COLLEGE APTITUDE OF STUDENTS

Several warnings must be expressed at the beginning of a discussion of aptitudes of college students. The first is that college aptitude tests in general are intended to measure only the student's ability to deal with abstract mathematical, or verbal concepts. Ability of this kind appears to be important in mastering the liberal arts curriculum, and aptitude tests allow one to make satisfactory statistical predictions of college success, even though they cannot identify which individual student will succeed and which will fail or give up. Instructors should be aware that student test scores usually available to them have not measured social ability, creative ability, talent in art or politics or music or athletics. They

[9]*Ibid.,* pp. 208-209.

do not assess the quality of student motivation, cultural background, or mental stability. College aptitude tests are valid and useful within their limitations, but they give only incomplete information at best. Their importance should be recognized but not overemphasized.

Furthermore, there is a considerable cultural bias in scores on college aptitude tests. Upper middle class high school graduates do better on them than do members of other social classes, largely because most of the testmakers come from that stratum. In addition, it is believed that youth from lower social classes are less likely to take tests seriously and to strive to do well on them. As concerted efforts are made to identify and to bring to college greater numbers of able youth from disadvantaged families, it will be more necessary to base estimates of ability on evidence other than aptitude test scores and high school grades. Imaginative effort will be required to bring the real aptitude of these students up to their potential aptitude.

A third warning in assessing student aptitude concerns the meaning of norms on standardized aptitude tests. Student performance on these tests is ordinarily reported to the instructor, if he asks, in percentile ranks or as some score that compares the individual student to a group of other students who have taken the test. The unwary instructor who hears that a student ranks "at the 50th percentile" may think he has been told that this student is an average high school graduate. This interpretation is almost certainly erroneous. Aptitude scores are usually reported in relation to groups of freshmen who have been admitted to college: the individual is compared to a selected group of the total population. Even with the great numbers of students now admitted to college, the average college aptitude of college freshmen is well above the average for the entire population. If expressed as intelligence quotients, the average mental ability of all college freshmen probably falls within the range 110 to 115; the lowest tenth of freshmen would score slightly below the average IQ of 100, in the range of the 90s. Unless some other comparison group is specified, the instructor is justified in assuming that percentile scores of his students on a college aptitude test refer to their rank among college freshmen in four-year liberal arts colleges. Table 1, derived from a report of *Project Talent*, compares the aptitude distributions of a sizeable group of high school graduates who entered college in 1960 with the distribution of scores for a group of like size drawn from graduates who did not enter college. High school dropouts, amounting to as many as one-third of the entire age group, are not included in either distribution. Seventy-nine percent of college entrants scored above the median

**TABLE 1.**

**Comparison of 1960 aptitude distributions for high school graduates who entered and did not enter college**

| Aptitude percentile rank | Percentage of high school graduates | |
|---|---|---|
| | Who entered college | Who did not enter college |
| 90.0–99.9 | 23 | 3 |
| 80.0–89.9 | 19 | 6 |
| 70.0–79.9 | 16 | 8 |
| 60.0–69.9 | 12 | 11 |
| 50.0–59.9 | 9 | 12 |
| 40.0–49.9 | 7 | 12 |
| 30.0–39.9 | 5 | 13 |
| 20.0–29.9 | 4 | 12 |
| 10.0–19.9 | 3 | 12 |
| 0.0– 9.9 | 2 | 11 |

Source: Richard Pearson, "Admission to College," in Earl J. McGrath (ed.), *Universal Higher Education.* New York: McGraw-Hill Book Company, 1966.

based on high school graduates; that entrants are a highly selected group is confirmed by the showing that only 40 percent of the nonentrant group scored above the median for high school graduates, a difference of 39 percent in the two distributions. It is worth noticing also that 5 percent of the college entrants were drawn from the lowest two deciles of the aptitude rankings of high school graduates.

Table 2 shows percentages of students who scored in each tenth of a national norm distribution for college freshmen on the American Council on Education Psychological Examination. Distributions are reported for several colleges with similar purposes. If students in each of these colleges had been exactly similar to the national norm group of students, 50 percent would earn scores below the 50th percentile and 25 and 75 percent, respectively, below the 25th and the 75th percentiles. If these students were exactly like the national norm group, 10 percent would earn scores in each of the ten categories. If the colleges were truly similar, their distributions of freshmen scores would be similar.

It is apparent that these six similar colleges report median scores differing by 23.6 percentile points (A and C) and that there is a true qualitative difference

**TABLE 2.**

**Percentages of freshman students in six 4-year colleges
earning ACE-test scores in given percentile ranges**

| Percentile range | Expected percentage | College | | | | | |
|---|---|---|---|---|---|---|---|
| | | A | B | C | D | E | F |
| 90–99 | 10 | 5 | 10 | 10 | 9 | 10 | 3 |
| 80–89 | 10 | 5 | 13 | 18 | 8 | 14 | 8 |
| 70–79 | 10 | 7 | 13 | 14 | 10 | 14 | 6 |
| 60–69 | 10 | 9 | 14 | 14 | 11 | 14 | 13 |
| 50–59 | 10 | 10 | 12 | 12 | 12 | 13 | 13 |
| 40–49 | 10 | 10 | 16 | 17 | 17 | 11 | 17 |
| 30–39 | 10 | 14 | 6 | 4 | 5 | 6 | 7 |
| 20–29 | 10 | 17 | 10 | 7 | 15 | 13 | 15 |
| 10–19 | 10 | 14 | 4 | 3 | 10 | 4 | 12 |
| 0–9 | 10 | 9 | 1 | 1 | 3 | 1 | 6 |
| Median | 50 | 40.0 | 60.2 | 63.6 | 49.8 | 60.9 | 45.4 |

The distributions are based on the same test given to freshmen in similar colleges in the same year. Since the identity of the colleges is not essential to the discussion, it is not reported here.

between the student bodies of these institutions. At the same time, it is evident that the ranges of ability in each institution cover the entire range of the norm group. There are "top" students in College A and some "poor" freshmen in College B. It is probable that instructors in both colleges will have students in the same class whose IQs differ by 40 points or more.

Several generalizations may be drawn from the small sample of aptitude data in Table 2. First, colleges differ—some much more widely than the six presented in the table. The ablest student in one college might even find himself in the lowest quarter of the ability distribution in another. Second, within any college, students will be found of quite different aptitudes. Third, in no college, and at no period in the history of higher education, are all the students drawn from the top ability levels. Finally, it is well to state once more the truism that, important as measured aptitude is in college success, aptitude accounts for only a part of the variance in college student achievement. Other personality factors can defeat exceptionally high aptitude or supplement mediocre aptitude.

**Figure 1-4.**
The transition of minority students from high school to college is facilitated by joint participation of college professors in special secondary school programs such as science field trips. (University of California, Santa Cruz)

New provisions for admission of selected minority group students who do not meet previous admission requirements raises questions about their eventual college success. In 1970, it is still too early to evaluate the benefit of irregular admission except in the most superficial numerical terms—after a year or two, so many are still in college, so many have dropped out after one or two semesters. There is indirect evidence, however, that significant numbers of high school graduates of average aptitude can become successful in college. The College of the Sequoias, one of the California community colleges, completed a study of the academic performance of the average ability student in California's university campuses and state colleges.

The College studied the academic performance of "average students" during the years 1953-54 to 1963-64—a total of 11 classes, involving 1,770 matriculants out of a total over the period of 10,311 freshmen. The "average ability" group constituted 17.17 percent of all admitted freshmen. For purposes of the study, "average students" were defined as those who met two criteria: (a) college aptitude test percentile rankings on published national norms between 40th and 60th percentiles; and (b) group tested IQ scores between 90 and 110. Only students meeting both criteria were included in the study.

Over the entire period, 32 percent of the entire "average" group graduated from College of the Sequoias with the Associate in Arts degree. In addition, some students transferred to other institutions without completing graduation requirements, and some successfully completed two years of study but did not take the degree. Achievement after transfer was calculated for only the first nine classes, since not enough time had elapsed at the time of the study for the 1962 and 1963 classes to earn the bachelor's degree. Of the 1,396 average students in those nine classes, 435 (32 percent) transferred to units of the University of California or of the California State Colleges; 234 of these had attained the bachelor's degree by 1964, and 11 were still in attendance. In percentages, 16.7 percent of all average entering students completed the four-year degree; graduates were 54 percent of the transfer group. The grade point average at the four-year college of the "average" transfer who graduated was 2.54. Non-graduates averaged only 2.20. The range of grade point averages for the entire transfer group of average students was from 0.79 to 3.84. Fifteen percent of the total transfer group fell below the 2.0 ("C") average; 9 percent averaged above 3.0 ("B").

The College of the Sequoias study concluded that its program did provide a proving ground for potential four-year college students of average aptitude; more than four-fifths of the transfer students were capable of adequate academic performance at four-year institutions. Although the study was not concerned primarily with students from minority groups, it provides basis for the theory that disadvantaged students of average ability may also be prepared to complete bachelor's degree study, granted that problems of finances, motivation, and opportunity are solved.

## THE GROWING COLLEGE POPULATION

The primary fact about college students today is their increase in numbers. Rising enrollments derive from three separate kinds of increases—in population, in proportion of the population graduating from high school, and in proportion of high school graduates who attend college. As a result of these compounded increases, the total degree-credit enrollments in colleges are twenty-nine times as large in 1970 as they were in 1900; a conservative projection indicates that by 1980 degree credit enrollments will reach 10 million. In that year, the large number of babies born in 1962 will reach the age of college entrance. Until 1980, continuing additions will be needed in both faculties and facilities for higher education.

### SOURCES OF GROWTH

The first line of Table 3 shows the first source of growth in college enrollments, the increase in the college entering age group. If nothing else had changed, the annual addition of as many as 1.5 million to earlier cadres of the seventeen-year-old college eligibles would bring an 80 percent increase in enrollments over a twenty-year period. The number of students entering in 1975 is expected to triple the number that enrolled in 1955. In addition to the fact that there are more persons in the age group, the proportion of youth who graduate from high school (and so meet minimum requirements for college entrance) will increase from 61 percent in 1955 to 89 percent in 1975. Finally, a 10 percent increase will take place in the proportion of the larger number of graduates who choose to go to college. So the problem of numbers continues to be compounded: higher proportions of high school graduates finding college educations not only necessary but desirable.

**TABLE 3.**

**Numbers of seventeen-year-olds, high school graduates,
and college enrollments, 1955 to 1975**

| Years | 1955 | 1960 | 1965 | 1970 | 1975 |
|---|---|---|---|---|---|
| youth 17 years old (1,000s) | 2,199 | 2,862 | 3,159 | 3,475 | 3,739 |
| h.s. grads. (1,000s) | 1,346 | 1,864 | 2,642 | 2,906 | 3,319 |
| grads./17s (%) | 61.2 | 65.1 | 83.6 | 83.6 | 88.7 |
| first-time enrollments (1,000s) | 670 | 923 | 1,442 | 1,676 | 1,990 |
| h.s. grads enrolled (%) | 49.7 | 49.5 | 54.6 | 57.7 | 59.9 |
| 17s who enroll (%) | 30.5 | 32.3 | 45.6 | 48.2 | 53.2 |

Source: *Health, Education and Welfare TRENDS,* 1967, and *Education in the Seventies,* 1968. Both: Washington: Government Printing Office.

### PERSISTENCE IN COLLEGE

The American college student group seems to be a comparatively unstable one. Its membership changes from term to term, as students enter, withdraw, transfer, are dropped, and reenter in response to influences either trivial or grave. It seems certain that only a minority of college freshmen are sternly dedicated to the task of achieving a diploma within four years, no matter what the odds may be. A majority of freshmen seem to enter into college careers lightly, tentatively, experimentally, uncertainly, without serious commitment either to an academic goal or to the institution they have chosen. Under these conditions, the concept of the college class loses much of its meaning and its sentimental attachment. "Class of '75" no longer signifies a group of old friends who have had common campus experiences and share common memories of professors, dormitories, athletic victories, and spring sings under the moonlit elms. It is difficult to develop a common loyalty simply on the basis of a common graduation ceremony.

Studies of persistence in college are summarized in *Beyond High School,*[10] a

[10] James W. Trent and Leland L. Medsker, *Beyond High School* (San Francisco: Jossey-Bass, Inc., 1968).

longitudinal survey of some 10,000 high school graduates of the year 1959. In their own study, that confirmed in general the findings of previous studies, Trent and Medsker found that

> Nearly half of the students who entered college full time in September, 1959, had withdrawn before June, 1963, and 23 percent of the students remained in college for four years without obtaining their baccalaureate degree, leaving 28 percent who obtained degrees within a conventional four-year period.[11]

Moreover, the highest rate of attrition occurred before the beginning of the student's second year in college:

> 49 percent of the withdrawals first left college before their second year of studies, 30 percent withdrew before their third year, 17 percent before their fourth year, and four percent during the fourth year . . . . From the interviews with the representative sample of these youths, it was evident that, although many of the withdrawals wanted to return to college, most of those who did indicate a desire to return expressed no hope of doing so in the foreseeable future.[12]

The high ratio of early withdrawal points up a serious problem for research in a period of growing enrollments. If nearly half of the students who attempt college withdraw before graduation, and an additional quarter require more than four years to earn a baccalaureate degree, should not colleges and universities be urgently concerned about identification of "freshmen most likely to complete"? Large numbers of competent students, already selected and admitted, withdraw from college voluntarily, or in response to obstacles that are largely nonacademic in nature. At the same time, other applicants are denied admission to their first choice college, and some competent students do not even apply. Is this situation inevitable? Is the waste involved inherent in a system of free choice? Could the identification and motivation for college of able high school students be improved? To what extent do the colleges themselves contribute to the dropout rate, especially that in the freshman year, by inadequate counseling, inappropriate curriculums, or ineffective teaching? Is a high rate of withdrawal an inescapable consequence of combining unlimited opportunity with exacting

[11] *Ibid.,* p. 78.
[12] *Ibid.,* p. 81.

academic standards? Until answers are available to questions of this kind, evaluation of withdrawal statistics will be difficult and ambiguous.

## ADDITIONAL ASPECTS OF THE STUDENT BODY

In addition to their increase in numbers and the rising proportions of able youth from minority groups who enter college, there are other significant characteristics of the American college student body. Men still outnumber women in college enrollments, although in recent years the proportion of women students has increased to about 45 percent. Some problems of college policy are posed, for instructors as well as for college administrations, by the increasing numbers of women in college classes and by the concomitant trend toward the disappearance of colleges for men only or for women only.

Studies of test performance and of school grades indicate that there are few differences in the native academic abilities of women and men. Nonetheless, it is also true that there are significant differences between men and women in their interests, ambitions, emotional reactions to aspects of learning and to academic competition, and occupational destinations. It is not exaggerated to state that the college woman is preparing for two careers—employment and homemaking—and the college man only for one. However, in most of our coeducational colleges women share a curriculum intended primarily for men and only partially and accidentally suited to the real needs of women. New instructors will have little influence in changing this pattern, but until some of them think deeply about it, there is no likelihood of change.

Married students, undergraduate as well as graduate, are increasing in numbers, so that it is no longer surprising for an instructor to have both husband and wife in one of his classes. An even more common pattern is for one spouse, usually the wife, to work while the other completes his degree. Mature women who have raised their youngest children to school age are another growing category of married students, as they prepare for a new career in order to help educate their families.

The age distribution of college students has changed drastically during the past quarter-century, partly as a result of increase in graduate enrollments, partly because people of all ages desire to improve their education and their level of employment. Although it is still customary to use the age groups of eighteen to

**Figure 1-5.**
The traditional concept of college represented by residential dormitory living has been greatly altered since World War II.

twenty-one or eighteen to twenty-four as the basis for discussion of college enrollment trends, fully one-fourth of all degree-credit students are twenty-five years old or over.

All of the developments mentioned have educational implications. In a residential college in which nearly all the students are of "college age," single, living in dormitories, and employed only at their studies or as student help around the campus, the instructor can assume, perhaps naively, that the primary preoccupation of his class is study. If a majority of students drive to class from their homes, if half are working half-time or more, if one-fourth are over twenty-five, and one-fourth are married, it is not wise to assume that their primary interests are on campus in college assignments and college activities. The greater average maturity of the freshman class indicates a greater seriousness of purpose and depth of understanding in the student body. Older students are more likely to be critical, argumentative, set in their opinions and prejudices, and so more challenging to the instructor. By the same token they may be less free to concentrate their whole attention on assignments and to center their values wholly on campus activities. These changes in student characteristics do not necessarily imply a lowering of standards or a deterioration in the role of the instructor, but they do require a modernization of the stereotypes of college life and college students.

## THE STUDENT AND COLLEGE PURPOSES

In response to changes in the makeup of the student body, the total system of higher education has changed. Old institutions have adjusted admission practices to admit women (or men), as well as to recruit applicants from minority groups or poverty cultures. New curriculums, even new colleges, have been established within existing universities to provide for newly realized educational needs. Almost every state has restudied its provisions for higher education, and entered on plans of expansion that include community colleges and newly established four-year colleges or universities. Patterns of faculty and student participation in operation and control of institutions are being evolved so as to make sure that those who are affected by policy are represented in its formation. New formulations define the relation of the student to the authority of the college; the old concept of *in loco parentis* is no longer applicable to the newer categories of students, and even the traditional categories rebel against being denied due process and the freedoms of their non-college agemates. All aspects of college operation have been called into question. Many of them are in transition, making changes that will alter the intrinsic nature of higher education in the decades ahead. Some of the serious problems that confront colleges in the decade of the seventies arise from the differences in goals as perceived by society, by faculty and administration, and by students.

### SOCIETY'S GOALS

Society's traditional expectations for the outcomes of higher education are affected by the history of higher education and by established patterns of founding and financial support of colleges. Concepts of academic standards and of equal opportunity are involved, as well as the practice of encouraging almost all young people to graduate from multi-purpose rather than specialized high schools. The diversity of higher education institutions makes an understanding of goals complex, as does the emergence of the "lifelong learning" movement. It would be difficult to draft a single concise statement of national goals for higher education.

One of the first modern attempts was that of the President's Commission on Higher Education, reporting to President Truman in December 1947. In six small volumes this commission considered the goals of higher education and a series of practical problems in equalizing opportunity and in organizing, staffing, and financing higher education.[13] In the light of its analysis, the Commission attempted to select those goals which should have first priority in our time. They are to bring to all the people of the nation:

Education for a fuller realization of democracy in every phase of living.

Education directly and explicitly for international understanding and cooperation.

Education for the application of creative imagination and trained intelligence to the solution of social problems and to the administration of public affairs.[14]

---

[13] The six volumes are bound as one in *Higher Education for American Democracy* (New York: Harper & Row, Publishers, Inc., 1948).

[14] *Ibid.*, vol. I., p. 8.

A decade later, the Educational Policies Commission of the National Education Association identified major purposes of American institutions of higher education, which may be summarized as follows:

1. To help realize the dream of individual opportunity, so that every young man and woman who is able to profit from post-high school education may have access to it.

2. To preserve and enrich the cultural heritage by developing programs related to social needs and to student interests, by emphasizing the social utility of education, and by pushing back the frontiers of knowledge.

3. To help provide solutions for society's problems by playing an active role in the transfer of learning to life.[15]

The two sets of purposes quoted are similar in many respects. They are echoed in other reports written by state and national committees or survey teams. There is no body that can prescribe to all American colleges, or pretend to express their unanimous view. Professors have objected to both of these reports because of their emphasis on the social responsibility and the applied values of higher education. It seems clear, nonetheless, that the purposes described are those that the American people expect their colleges and universities to achieve. No matter how dedicated they may be to pure research and to unfettered scholarship, the faculties of higher education must also consider these goals for "the second echelon of intellectuality."

The national interest as expressed in legislation emphasizes *individual opportunity for the fullest development of the talents of every citizen.* The nation expects that arrangements will be developed to permit every young person to pursue education to the full extent of his ability and his desire, without artificial limitation or discrimination. A corollary of this principle is the belief that all human talents that are necessary to the well-being of the community are worthy of respect, that complete and appropriate education of the technician is important for society in the same way as is the complete and appropriate education of the professor or the physician or the philosopher. In the American view, if the education of any category of workers is neglected or despised, the society suffers.

---

[15] Educational Policies Commission, *Higher Education in a Decade of Decision* (Washington: National Education Association, 1957), pp. 6-10.

*Education for civic responsibility* is a second national purpose of colleges, one that is not primary among the objectives of the faculty or of the student. The quotation from George Washington's Farewell Address expresses the point forcefully: "Promote then, as an object of primary importance, institutions for the general diffusion of knowledge. In proportion as the structure of a government gives force to public opinion, it is essential that public opinion be enlightened."[16]

In addition to the task of acquainting the student with the history and values of his culture, the college is expected to prepare him to act responsibly in discussing and in exercising choices in political, sociological, and economic affairs of both national and international scope.

*The preparation of talented workers for the economy* is a third national expectation of higher education. In certain vocations, notably the ministry and the bar, the colleges shared responsibility for this purpose from the beginning. During the nineteenth century, the preparation of physicians, scientists, and teachers was introduced to the campus. The foundation of the land-grant colleges added a strong emphasis on the practical applications of knowledge, so that the role of the college in preparing agricultural extension workers, veterinarians, engineers, businessmen, dentists, nurses, or librarians is unquestioned. At present, the conflict between the conservative forces of the academic faculties and national expectations centers about the propriety of college courses for technical workers such as occupational therapists, psychiatric technicians for mental hospitals, dental hygienists, and engineering assistants. In this conflict as in previous ones dealing with the expansion of college services, it is probable that the needs of the economy will prevail.

*The national interest in research* adds a practical side to the professor's dedication to fundamental inquiry. Not only are industrial laboratories seeking profitable applications of new insights into nature, but higher education, too, is concerned with the utility of its laboratory discoveries. The marked increase in agricultural productivity over the past century derives in large part from research in the land-grant colleges. The development of atomic energy, the exploration of the uses of radioactive isotopes, the virtual eradication of poliomyelitis, and chemical approaches to the treatment of mental diseases all derive from university applications of principles discovered in university laboratories.

Finally, the nation expects its colleges and universities *to be responsive to*

---

[16] Saxe Commins (ed.), *Basic Writings of George Washington* (New York: Random House, Inc., 1948), pp. 637-638.

**Figure 1-6.**
Society's continuing interest in extending the frontiers of knowledge in all fields encourages professorial research.

*emerging educational needs,* broadly defined. Existing agencies may resist the addition of new purposes and so diminish their contact with and their value to the dynamic society that supports them. If they do, other establishments will be created to carry on new educational endeavors, with resulting conflict, inefficiency, and fossilization of the older institutions. On the other hand, the nearly 2,500 colleges and universities of the United States can dedicate themselves to continuing service to the nation by taking the lead in recognizing new educational needs and in developing defensible and realistic programs to meet those needs. They may seek an evanescent security by clinging to tradition and resisting growth; or they may attain permanent influence by careful analysis of trends and scholarly direction of the needed changes.

### GOALS OF THE FACULTY

The faculty defines the goals of higher education somewhat less pragmatically than does society. Especially in recent decades, the faculty rejects the idea that the university is an instrument to be manipulated for national goals. Rather, the university is considered to be an independent entity, seeking to shape its own nature through continuing efforts to know, to understand, and to interpret. Utilitarian applications of its discoveries and insights or extrinsic determination of its priorities are resisted as unworthy distractions from the true functions of the scholar. There is a danger, in this view, to the independence of the university and to the search for truth if the university is too closely associated with the problems and the transitory crises of the outside world. For example, a study of 1,600 faculty members at ten leading graduate schools found that only 5 percent favored social involvement, 14 percent "believed scholars should remain detached from social problems," and "81 percent believed that the scholar's role is to seek knowledge basic to the needs of mankind and provide education in intellectual analysis for those who will bring about social improvement."[17]

The teaching responsibility of the college is accepted and even treasured by some professors. Yet one cause of campus unrest is surely the conflict between the reluctance of the faculty to teach and the demand of the young to be taught. Official statements found in college and university catalogs tend to combine the two purposes, and yet are so broad and abstract that they are not of immediate value in developing the activities of the faculty. The implicit ideal of the university, memories of impressive teachers, and convictions about standards within each discipline are more important in determining the concrete activities of the faculty than are closely reasoned philosophic positions.

It is probable that the faculties of American colleges and universities would agree in the broadest terms on three basic purposes. First and foremost, they see themselves as scholars, and they conceive that their efforts should be devoted to the extension, through research, of understanding in all areas of knowledge. Second, the scholar feels a responsibility to identify, to recruit, and to guide those who will continue research in the future. For this reason he accepts the education of scholars in his field as an integral purpose. Since he recognizes that not all students will wish to specialize in his discipline, he accepts a third purpose, that of the liberal education of the nonspecialist. Through liberal education he hopes to contribute to the continuous selection of a trained elite from which the nation's leadership may come.

[17] American Association for Higher Education, *College and University Bulletin* 21, no. 10 (March 1, 1969): p. 3.

## STUDENT EXPECTATIONS

These specialized purposes of the faculty group are at many points in conflict with the implicit and intuitive but powerful purposes of the students and their parents. The student sees college education as a source of economic advantage. He hopes to be trained professionally so that he can earn more money than he could without a college degree and to be sharpened in his competitive skills. This purpose may be unworthy, even unrealistic, but it is an important factor in encouraging young people to seek education beyond the high school. Even more vaguely, perhaps, the student anticipates that the college will provide him with intellectual excitement and challenge, that he will be stimulated to achieve understanding and to love learning. Too often this student purpose finds only a token counterpart in the efforts and the attitudes of the professor. Thirdly, the student expects the college to contribute to all aspects of personal development, through health services, counseling offices, placement services, social training in group living, student activities, and sports. Convinced that the college has extensive responsibility for all aspects of his development, the student finds himself at odds with the professor who desires to limit his influence to intellectual growth only.

Harold Taylor has expressed the point of view of many of the newer recruits to higher education:[18]

If they are ignorant, what they need is knowledge, not exclusion from further education; if they have not yet learned to learn, if their environment has crushed their curiosity, if they are culturally undernourished, if their vocabulary is underdeveloped, what they need is teaching which is lively, vigorous, informed, and productive; they need a chance to get started, not more hours of textbook material they can't yet handle. If their test scores are low, what they need is a teacher who can find out why and can set about raising them, not someone who classifies them as stupid on the basis of circumstantial evidence. If their teachers are incompetent what they need is better teaching, not a storm of rhetoric against American education . . . . The curriculum will contain those studies and will foster those experiences which are significant in the individual lives of the students and are at the same time relevant to the

---

[18]Harold Taylor, "The American Idea," in *Current Issues in Higher Education, 1960,* ed. G. Kerry Smith (Washington: American Association for Higher Education, 1960), pp. 44-46.

needs of society in which the students will live . . . . We therefore need to concentrate our national attention on the proposition that a free society in a free world can only be achieved when our educational system has not only taught its citizens the skills and techniques necessary to run a modern industrial society, but has taught them to believe in the generosity of heart, the boldness of imagination, and the liberal ideals of a truly democratic philosophy.

## A DIVERSITY OF GOALS

From this discussion of function and purpose of American higher education, several statements can be made. In the first place, it is clear that American colleges and universities have accepted not just one, but a variety of purposes. Even though some of these purposes compete with each other for the support of the public, for the attention of the faculty, and for the time of the student, all are important, and all are likely to be permanent. A consequence of this variety of purposes is a diversity of institutions. Universities, institutes, colleges, seminaries, academies, teachers colleges, and junior colleges, whether public or private, residential or commuting, experimental, traditional, or undecided—all share in a responsibility for liberal education, and each assumes one or more specialized areas of professional or occupational education.

Diversity of purposes implies, second, a hierarchy of goals for higher education, some so essential and fundamental that they must be adopted by every college. The preservation, enhancement, and transmission of the culture is an example of this sort of purpose. More specific aims may be adopted or rejected by each college, in harmony with the college's own view of its role; they are not essential elements of the definition of a college. The professional education of physicians or barristers or teachers is an example of these more specific purposes; professional education extends the scope of higher education but is not a necessary part of it. In addition, there is a third level of accidental purposes of institutions; efforts to achieve these ends may strengthen the other goals or interfere with them. They are peripheral in the sense that any embellishment is peripheral—pleasant to have if it can be afforded, but not truly essential to the operation. The purposes of student activities and of student personnel services fall within this category.

The two considerations just presented, of the diversity and of the classification of objectives, apply specifically to colleges and universities. A third conclusion is that these institutions exist in a culture that fosters and supports them and that inevitably controls them at least in part. The purposes of higher education in America cannot be stated frankly and realistically without recognition of some of the elements of that culture. For example, the purposes of American higher education are affected by the development of technology. The higher standard of living frees a larger proportion of the population to pursue higher education for longer periods. The technology that produces that standard of living has an insatiable appetite for workers with the skill to control it and the understanding to extend it.

Fourth, growing student populations cannot be ignored in a consideration of purposes. The ivory tower of learning, frequented only by noble minds intent on the mastery of all knowledge and its extension through dedicated research, is a charming and attractive fantasy. The college teacher of the late twentieth century must abandon this dream. The reality is that half of all high school graduates need, desire, and will have an opportunity to attend further schooling. The purposes of higher education must include not only the immediate goals of the students, but their introduction to the world of ideas and to the excitement of intellectual discovery.

Fifth, the culture embraces both idealistic aspirations as well as material production and rising birthrates. The American dream of upward social mobility by means of education has proved historically true and is a powerful source of individual motivation. Higher education must recognize this element also in its statement of purposes.

The emergence of these recent influences on the purposes of higher education has not invalidated earlier emphases in American colleges and universities on the liberal education of the student and on the extension of knowledge through research. A sixth conclusion is that new conditions in the sustaining culture have not substituted one set of purposes for another; they have added new ones. As a result, older institutions have become more complex as they add new functions; and new institutions have been established to achieve some of the newly-emerging purposes. This continuing process of reevaluation and adaptation accounts for the complexity of the system of higher education and of the individual units within the system.

## STANDARDS OF STUDENT ACHIEVEMENT

The question of academic standards for higher education seems to be a classic dilemma, in that neither ruthless selectivity nor surrender to mass methods is acceptable. If college doors could be closed to all but the most able 3 or 5 or even 10 percent of college age youth and if all but the most eager scholars could be disqualified early in the course, standards would seem secure. At least the student would not be an obstacle to a curriculum emphasizing breadth of culture, depth of understanding, and height of abstraction. Although this manner of selection has been practiced in the European universities, it is not clear that the results for society and for individual students have been uniformly good. In America, the national spirit requires that opportunity for education be made available to all who can possibly benefit from it, and the momentum of our technology depends upon a labor force with a high average of educated skill and understanding. The attainment of high standards through elimination of applicants is therefore an unacceptable solution of the dilemma.

The solution of despair is equally repellent. Dismayed at the prospect of doubling and tripling the numbers of college students, some instructors fear that the only possible curriculum will be a series of superficial, watered-down, lowest-common-denominator surveys of knowledge. From such fare, they hope, a few of the ablest students may be surreptitiously segregated for special demanding and challenging programs. This also is a fraudulent solution to the dilemma. No one—society, students, the educational system, or the unhappy professors—could profit from this degradation of scholarship. Some alternative to these two extremes, not necessarily a middle ground or compromise, but perhaps an entirely fresh solution must be found.

A first step in the defense of standards would be a thorough scrutiny of the curriculum, course by course, and of each course, topic by topic, with a view to eliminating the unnecessary, the trivial, the antiquated, and the simply untrue. The college curriculum is one of the most stable elements in American life. Additions are made to it, but rarely is a course or a discipline eliminated. Students increase and courses increase and faculty numbers decrease; the need for some adjustment is apparent. The question of Herbert Spencer, "What knowledge is of most worth?" was never more pressing. Some choice must be made. It is better to teach one topic thoroughly, deeply, rigorously, with due attention to its importance in life, rather than teach seven or eight topics superficially and hurriedly.[19]

An obvious step in the improvement of standards would be to lengthen the

---

[19]Earl J. McGrath, *Memo to a College Faculty Member* (New York: Teachers College, Bureau of Publications, 1961).

average time spent in study. This step aggravates the problem of too many students for too few professors, but it does allow the students a chance to master a greater share of extant scholarship. This lengthening of the years of study is, in fact, occurring. More youth graduate from high school, and more of the graduates enter college. In many fields, the bachelor's degree in fact takes four and a half or five years of study rather than four. In addition, more and more graduates go on to begin graduate work. Thus, the period of economic dependence is prolonged and the student achieves a longer education, but not necessarily one of improved quality.

Programs of independent study for students at all levels of aptitude and sophistication show some promise of improving the quality of higher education. Colleges that have experimented with these plans emphasize that their main purpose is not economy of money or of faculty time, but a return to the student of the responsibility for his education. Ability and interest in further study are accepted as qualities desired in the college graduate. Independent study programs are intended to give the student practice in the skills of learning so that these qualities may be achieved.

Concern with the quality of teaching is another aspect of the improvement of standards; the teacher as well as the student contributes to the quality of learning. The instructor must be aware that some student failures may be caused by his own ineptitude, rather than by student incalcitrance when faced with the challenge of excellent, inspiring, and demanding instruction. Few students reject competent teaching; none should be judged unworthy of it.

Finally, the question of standards is involved both in the trend toward recruitment of able minority group students whose preparation for college study is deficient, and in the student quest for relevance in education. It is no longer acceptable for colleges simply to refuse admission to students (who need further education as an essential first step in their progress toward social and economic equality) on the grounds that they have not been prepared to compete academically. It is equally unacceptable to admit them only to disqualify them at the first grading period because they have not found anything in the curriculum that seems worth their attention.

An ideal solution to this problem of preparation for college will be achieved when lower schools are enabled to provide excellent education for all American children, and when the children are able to have equal access to it. While that goal is being worked on, an intermediate school may be desirable, designed to enable young men and women to achieve the skills of learning by intensive study, so that they may later compete successfully in college curriculums. During most of the present decade, neither of these solutions is realistic for most of the deprived youth. High quality in the college education of this new category of students will be measured by the success of the colleges in developing programs that challenge their interest and enable them to achieve a competitive level of study skills and communicative ability. The system of higher education must emphasize the function of developing the talents of each individual, rather than simply screening a limited number of favored persons for the development of a limited range of learning.

Relevance is also a component of the standards of achievement. No matter how difficult and demanding a subject may be, it does not contribute to the quality of a student's education if it has little or no relation to his present or future activities. But to say so little is to beg the question, "What knowledge is most relevant?" The cry for relevance seems to be concerned most with liberal or general education, with curriculums intended to deal with personal and social and cosmic concerns. Students in professional schools—engineering, business, science, education, medicine—seem to accept in general the curriculums provided, partly because they see that graduates are successful in getting jobs. The same students are likely to criticize their liberal courses because they expect of them an immediacy and an applicability similar to those found in practical studies.

The solution does not seem to lie in allowing students to determine entirely what they choose to study. Attempts to convince them by "hard-sell" techniques of the value of traditional subject matter and teaching procedures are equally ineffective solutions. A cooperative effort is needed, so that students and professors may negotiate in good faith to develop the broad directions and to choose specific content for general education. Youth's concern about its own education can become a priceless stimulant to the kind of involvement in education that begets high quality. Conditions of life have changed drastically and will continue to change: higher education must help students to understand and in part to direct those changes. This is the meaning of relevance.

## SUMMARY

American higher education continues its evolution in response to social forces that have not previously affected the college curriculum. A rising standard of living, a sophisticated technology, a closer interrelationship among all nations, a doubling and redoubling in the numbers of college students, and an increased concern of students with the educational aspects of college life have combined to cause a reexamination of the purposes of higher education. New emphasis is being placed on widespread availability of higher education that will be of significance to students, relevant to the needs of American society, and creative in extending the boundaries of knowledge and wisdom. The importance of each of these major purposes has led to the development of a variety of institutions of higher education, some emphasizing only one of the aspects, whether teaching or research, and others striving to achieve notably in all three areas.

Diversity of curriculum within institutions is encouraged also by the competition of three points of view on the nature of college education—those of the faculty, the students, and the supporting society. In America, higher education has not been encouraged to exist and develop apart from the daily struggles of life. The scholar has been called on to exert an expert and responsible leadership in political and commercial affairs. Because of this emphasis on practicality and involvement, the American college or university has been and appears likely to remain an institution quite different from the European model.

This difference is reflected not only in the curriculum. It leads to a conviction, deeply ingrained in American thought, that no able youth shall be excluded from college by his inability to afford it. It leads to constantly increasing costs in colleges and universities. And it leads to a reconsideration of the concept of standards that is founded solely on the degree of abstraction of the subject matter presented.

In brief, American higher education faces several important issues. Among these are its availability to students, the definition of its curriculums, the quality of instruction, the evaluation of its accomplishments, the extent of institutional diversity, the conservation of exceptional talent, and appropriate patterns of financial support.

America has attempted to make higher education more widely available to its young people than any society has ever done before. There are pressing reasons why further expansion of educational opportunity should be encouraged, and at the same time there are serious problems that must be solved if this expansion is to be purposeful and orderly. The college professor can perform his many tasks more effectively if he is sensitive to these trends and aware of their implications.

## RELATED READING

Aston, Alexander W. *The College Environment.* Washington: American Council on Education, 1968.

Barzun, Jacques. *The American University.* New York: Harper and Row, 1968.

Baskin, Samuel (ed.). *Higher Education: Some Newer Developments.* New York: McGraw-Hill Book Company, 1965.

Butz, Otto. *To Make A Difference.* New York: Harper and Row, 1967.

Eurich, Alvin C. (ed.). *Campus 1980: The Shape of the Future in American Higher Education.* New York: Delacorte Press, 1968.

Dennis, Lawrence, and Joseph Kauffman (eds.). *The College and the Student.* Washington: American Council on Education, 1966.

Dobbin, Charles G., and Calvin B. T. Lee (eds.). *Whose Goals for American Higher Education?* Washington: American Council on Education, 1968.

Feuer, L. S. *Conflict of Generations.* New York: Basic Books, 1968.

Harcleroad, Fred F. (ed.). *Issues of the Seventies: The Future of Higher Education,* San Francisco: Jossey-Bass Publishers, 1970.

Kenniston, Kenneth. *The Uncommitted.* New York: Harcourt, Brace and World, 1965.

Minter, W. John (ed.). *The Individual and the System.* Boulder, Colo.: Western Interstate Institute on Higher Education, 1967.

Muscatine, Charles (ed.). *Education at Berkeley.* Report of the Select Committee on Education. Berkeley: University of California Press, 1968.

Nowlis, Vincent, Kenneth E. Clarke, and Miriam Rock. *The Graduate Student as Teacher.* Washington: American Council on Education, 1968.

Raushenbush, Esther. *The Student and His Studies.* Middletown, Conn.: Wesleyan University Press, 1964.

Sanford, Nevitt (ed.). *The American College.* New York: John Wiley and Sons, Inc., 1962.

——— *College and Character: A Briefer Version of The American College.* New York: John Wiley and Sons, Inc., 1964.

——— *Where Colleges Fail: A Study of the Student as a Person.* San Francisco: Jossey-Bass, Inc., 1968.

Taylor, Harold. *Students Without Teachers: The Crisis in the University.* New York: McGraw-Hill Book Company, 1969.

Thornton, James W., Jr. *The Community Junior College.* New York: John Wiley and Sons, Inc., 1966.

Woodring, Paul.*The Higher Learning in America: A Reassessment.* New York: McGraw-Hill Book Company, 1968.

Yamamoto, Kaoru. *The College Student and His Culture: An Analysis.* Boston: Houghton Mifflin Company, 1968.

# chapter two / THE COLLEGE PROFESSOR /

WHO ARE COLLEGE INSTRUCTORS? • THE PREPARATION OF COLLEGE TEACHERS • PROFESSIONAL RESPONSIBILITIES OF THE COLLEGE TEACHER • CONDITIONS OF WORK • ACADEMIC FREEDOM • THE INSTRUCTOR AND PROFESSIONAL SOCIETIES • THE INSTRUCTOR IN SEARCH OF A POSITION • SUMMARY • RELATED READING

The college student of the sixties will be the college professor of the seventies. It is likely that many of the generalizations that described the professor in the past will no longer apply. A recent study at the Center for Research and Development in Higher Education at the University of California at Berkeley was concerned with the attitudes of 1,200 of the doctoral students at ten "most prestigious" graduate schools; many of the respondents to this part of the study have already joined the teaching ranks.

Two paragraphs in a summary report of the study[1] indicate the nature of the predicted change:

> The point at issue—whether the traditionally socializing influences of academia will transform the newcomers into its image, or whether the institution's outlook and outreach will be revamped by their presence—has profound implications for the future of higher education. The chances are that both individuals and institutions will change. The young faculty member will doubtless assume some of the traditional academic values. And the institution may forsake some.

[1] Ann M. Heist, "Today's Graduate Student—Tomorrow's Faculty Member." *A.A.U.P. Bulletin* 55(1969):452-454. Reprinted from *The Research Reporter.* Berkeley: University of California, Center for Research and Development in Higher Education 5, no. 2(1969):5-7.

According to their responses in this study, the new and prospective faculty members opt for change in the university—even for radical change in some areas—but they have respect, by and large, for what the university system has accomplished, and are not bent on uprooting that system. Rather, they want to see it structurally modified and substantively strengthened as a center for learning.

As a part of his preparation for entry into the existing ranks of college professors, the new recruit can profit from a consideration of some of the conditions of academic life, so that he may understand the extent and the importance of the segment of the labor force to which he aspires. What opportunities for employment will there be in the near future? What are the usual conditions of work load and salary? How have professors been prepared for their work, and how do they find positions? What are their responsibilities and their privileges? These and related aspects of the life of the instructor are the concern of Chapter Two.

## WHO ARE COLLEGE INSTRUCTORS?

Literary and journalistic descriptions of college professors convey contradictory and confusing images of this rare species, numbering less than 0.2 percent of the population. These descriptions may subtly foster the frontiersman's distrust of the man who does not labor with his hands, or idealize the role of the searcher for truth and the molder of youth. One part of the national image is expressed in stories of "absentmindedness," told perhaps by the same person who, a moment later, will excoriate the "leftist radical brain-trusting eggheads." A lady may avoid the professor socially, fearing that her every utterance will be criticized and corrected. Another person will assume that the professor is a source of expert information on all subjects, simply because he is a college professor. (This layman is a danger chiefly because the professor is so willing to accept his evaluation!) Variations and contradictions in the stereotypes confirm the observation that there is no single professorial type but that as a class the professors exert an influence on the culture out of proportion to their numbers.

Professors, of course, function in many roles. Increasingly they are being lured from the campus to serve as corporation directors, government officials, industrial consultants, or full-time research workers. At one time, the decision to

**Figure 2-1.**
College professors, who comprise only a small percentage of the country's total population, exert an influence on the culture out of all proportion to their numbers.

work for a doctorate involved a lifetime commitment to teaching. Now, the decision need never be final; the professor often combines several careers or alternates between teaching and work in another field.

This new competition for professorial competence has several educational consequences, not all desirable. Contact with practical affairs may help to keep instruction timely; the opportunity for choice of occupation may aid in raising teaching salaries to more realistic levels. Negatively, the exodus from the campus makes it far more difficult to find all the fully qualified instructors that will be needed. This increases the difficulty for the graduate student to complete his advanced study, since his adviser is so frequently away. As a result of these two effects it is possible that the quality of instruction may deteriorate simply because there are not enough fully trained people to fill all the positions in all aspects of the economy.

The multiple roles of the professor suggest another observation about variety within the academic personality, namely, that there is no such thing as an ideal college teacher. Even within a single discipline, professors are needed with the abilities to interpret the material, to recruit majors for the subject, to extend knowledge through research, to administer affairs, and to apply their specialized knowledge to human problems. These abilities occur in an infinite number of combinations, as do other traits of personality that may make a teacher effective. Good teachers have been found among the choleric, the sanguine, the bilious, and the melancholic, to use an ancient classification. The significant variable in effective college teaching seems to be not so much health or knowledge, but rather a conviction that teaching is a task of such social and personal importance that every class hour deserves careful preparation. College graduates of most varied qualities can become effective college teachers, but their effectiveness will depend fundamentally on their determination to achieve competence through continuous effort.

A brief statistical statement will illustrate the problem of maintaining the numbers and the quality of the faculties of American colleges and universities. Table 1 sets forth the numbers of full-time-equivalent instructional staff, actual or projected, in resident instruction at intervals over a twenty-year period, the total full-time-equivalent opening enrollments in colleges and universities during those years, and the student-faculty ratios based on those numbers.

The study from which Table 1 was derived forecasts an annual need for new

**TABLE 1.**

**Full-time-equivalent instructional staff for resident degree-credit courses, and full-time-equivalent opening fall enrollment in institutions of higher education, 1955 to 1975**

| Year | F-T-E faculty | F-T-E opening fall enrollments | Student-faculty ratios |
|---|---|---|---|
| 1955-56 | 161,322 | 2,208,000 | 13.7 |
| 1960-61 | 210,000 | 2,943,000 | 14.0 |
| 1965-66 | 306,000 | 4,667,000 | 15.2 |
| 1970-71 | 388,000 | 6,142,000 | 15.8 |
| 1975-76 | 454,000 | 7,551,000 | 16.7 |

Source: Kenneth A. Simon and Marie G. Fullam, *Projection of Educational Statistics to 1975-76* (1966 Edition). Washington: Government Printing Office, 1966.

full-time-equivalent instructors, rising from the approximately 28,000 who were needed in 1960 to 43,000 instructors, and a total full-time-equivalent faculty (for resident and non-resident courses) of 533,000 for the year 1975-76. The forecast assumes that the student-faculty ratio in resident instruction will increase to about 16.7 to 1 by 1975.[2] The effect of this growth on the level of preparation of new faculty members can be seen from the disparity between the numbers of doctorates granted annually and the numbers of new teachers needed. In 1959-60, 9,800 doctorates were granted, but there was need for 28,000 new instructional staff. The total supply of doctorates will increase in the near future; for the projected 1975 need of 43,000 new instructors, the number of doctorates to be available is estimated at 36,000. Since only about 60 percent of newly prepared doctorates who change their occupations enter education, the actual numbers of new, fully trained teachers will continue to be much smaller than the need. If competition by industry and government for holders of advanced degrees intensifies, the net proportion of faculty who hold the doctorate degree will decline even further.

Several conclusions may be drawn from the statistics presented. It seems evident that the supply of graduate students and of doctoral degrees can become sufficient to maintain present levels of faculty training only if the occupation is made more attractive than competing occupations. In part, this attractiveness will come from salary levels competitive with those offered in industry. For all college teachers, the median annual salaries in 1967-68 ranged from $7,458 for instructors to $14,713 for professors.[3] There are marked variations in medians from one region to another and between classes of institutions, but very few colleges and universities offer beginning salaries that really compete with those in industry or even in government. Salaries in higher education increased by about 70 percent over the medians reported in 1957-58, but they have not quite kept pace with the increasing incomes of other professionally trained occupational groups.

Other suggestions for meeting the increased need for college teachers include

[2] Kenneth A. Simon and Marie G. Fullam, *Projections of Educational Statistics to 1975-76*, 1966 edition (Washington: Government Printing Office, 1966), Table 31.

[3] Research Division–National Education Association, *Economic Status of the Teaching Profession, 1967-68*. Research Report 1968-R4. (Washington: National Education Association, 1968). *Average* annual salaries reported by the American Association of University Professors (*A.U.U.P. Bulletin*, 54, no. 2 (Summer 1968): 197) are somewhat higher, partly because of a different base of reporting institutions.

the recruitment of greater numbers of women, the extension of the retirement age, greater use of part-time teachers from business and industry in the local community, increased effort by present faculty members to interest their ablest students in teaching, and more effective use of available faculty by means of independent study techniques and programmed instruction. Increase in supply from any of these sources would be a long-term project rather than an emergency measure.

Eckert, Stecklein, and Sagen investigated the motivations of college teachers in Minnesota. Their findings indicated that very often the decision to teach at the college level was reached almost accidentally and most frequently after graduation from college. Only 37 percent indicated that they had considered teaching in college while still undergraduates. Fully half had never really aspired to be college teachers and found themselves in that career as the result of chance occurrences. These teachers either came to college work from lower schools or had prepared for other careers but were invited to teach instead. The authors conclude that "the large number of people who characterized their entry to this field as accidental underscores the need to challenge promising students who are apparently bound for other careers, or who are still undecided about their life work."[4]

## THE PREPARATION OF COLLEGE TEACHERS

One of the most persistent—and seemingly most futile—discussions in American higher education deals with more effective preparation of college teachers. The conventional viewpoint holds that the ideal program is one that leads to the Ph.D. degree, even though less than half of all college and university teachers hold any doctoral degree. The other side of the argument admits the necessity of deep scholarship and the ability of the college teacher to do creative research, but insists that other qualities are also important and should be cultivated during the course of planned preparation for college teaching.

The proposal for the "doctorate-plus" has had a long history and eloquent advocates. William James wrote an essay on "The Ph.D. Octopus," and Jacques

[4] Ruth E. Eckert, John E. Stecklein, and H. Bradley Sagen, "College Faculty Members View Their Jobs," *A.A.U.P. Bulletin* 45(1959):512-528.

**Figure 2-2.**
College teaching is undergoing considerable change. Long distance telephone connections, now common between many main and branch campuses, place new and unfamiliar responsibilities upon those participating in each location. (Pennsylvania State University)

Barzun devoted a chapter to the same topic,[5] remarking in the course of it, "The doctorate of course shows nothing about teaching ability." In a discussion on the topic "Is the Present Ph.D. the Best Degree for College Teachers?" William C. DeVane remarked, "Obviously, it is not the ideal teaching degree, and many of our graduate schools insist that it is not primarily a teaching degree, but rather a degree for other, more general purposes."[6]

A recent statement in the same vein catalogs a few of the shortcomings imputed to college teachers, and by implication suggests some elements of a more complete program for their preparation.

> Perhaps in no regard are new college teachers more deficient than in their lack of insight into the nature of the college teaching profession. They lack even the rudimentary concepts of the ethics of the profession and appear to lack workable hypotheses about the balance of freedom and responsibility which ought to be characteristic of their field of endeavor. Their understanding of the nature of academic freedom is extremely limited, and they are often unprepared to establish satisfactory professional relationships with their faculty colleagues, with the administrators of the colleges, and, perhaps most of all, with the students they teach. They have no adequate perception of the variety of American colleges and the diverse purposes they serve. Their first professional position is often, therefore, accepted without a clear recognition of the obligations to which they should be committing themselves in the particular college in which they accept a position.[7]

Among observers who have written and spoken on the preparation of college teachers, a consensus seems to have been reached that the depth of knowledge implied in the doctorate is an essential quality of the effective college teacher, but that it is not of itself enough. Additional qualities must be developed before the man who has learned thoroughly becomes a man who can teach competently.

A good many professors object to the last statement. They are likely to suggest defensively that it implies a substitution of educational method for

[5] Jacques Barzun, *Teacher in America* (Garden City, New York: Doubleday and Company, Inc., 1954), chap. 14. (Paperback edition.)

[6] Joseph Axelrod (ed.), *Graduate Study for Future College Teachers* (Washington: American Council on Education, 1959), p. 7.

[7] W. Max Wise, "Who Teaches the Teachers?" in *Improving College Teaching,* ed. Calvin B.T. Lee (Washington: American Council on Education, 1967), p. 80.

substantive scholarship. They point to the fact that excellent teachers in the past had no training in methodology, as a proof of their contention that good teachers are born, not made. This partial truth obscures the fact that good teachers are not now born in sufficient numbers, or else they are drawn into other work. The fatalistic disclaimer seems, in addition, to cast doubt on the power of intelligent humans to acquire any skill at all. If men must be born, not taught, to teach, is not eugenics the only source also of doctors, lawyers, mathematicians, chemists, preachers, or philosophers?

Since the testimony of college presidents and of college freshmen indicates that present programs of preparation frequently fail to produce acceptable competence in college teaching, several plans are suggested for improved training. Among these are separate doctorates for the teacher and for the researcher in each discipline; a revitalization of the master's degree as a teaching degree; the establishment of an intermediate degree based on two years of graduate study; or a conscious effort to plan that all doctoral candidates undergo meaningful and supervised experience in teaching, instead of the more haphazard teaching assistantships that are now available only to a fraction of all future college teachers.

In a summary of viewpoints developed during his nationwide study of graduate education,[8] Berelson presented at a conference a dozen theses about the preparation of college teachers, from which five are quoted in part:[9]

(4) The recurring proposal of two doctoral degrees—one for college teachers and one for researchers—is undesirable.

(5) The master's degree should not and cannot be restored as a central degree for college teachers.

(6) The proposal of a new, intermediate two-year degree for college teachers might be worth a try but probably would not work well.

(7) Efforts to get "greater breadth" into doctoral programs are not likely to succeed.

(8) The training in teaching provided by the graduate school at the doctoral level is deficient and can be improved.

[8] Bernard Berelson, *Graduate Education in the United States* (New York: McGraw-Hill Book Company, Inc., 1960).

[9] John W. Gustad (ed.), *Faculty Preparation and Orientation* (Winchester, Mass.: New England Board of Higher Education, 1960), pp. 47-54.

In his elaboration of the eighth thesis, Berelson suggests that every doctoral candidate undergo at least a year of half-time teaching, actively supervised and systematically varied in subject matter, and that the candidate be required to participate in a seminar on the character and problems of the liberal arts college. No unanimity of informed opinion is available on this problem. It seems evident to informed observers that the quality of college teaching must be improved, but little concrete change has been reported during the decade since Berelson's proposals—nor indeed during the seven decades since William James raised the question. As a modest first step, Berelson's proposal deserves to be tried; at least it would serve to identify those of the doctoral candidates who had been "born" to be teachers and perhaps to eliminate from teaching those who could not be "made" into acceptable instructors.

## PROFESSIONAL RESPONSIBILITIES OF THE COLLEGE TEACHER

Competence as a college teacher depends on the acceptance by the teacher of several kinds of responsibility. The farmer or the factory worker may be intransigent and irresponsible, but the professor can rarely divest himself of the obligations imposed by his advanced learning, by his position as an exemplar, by his membership in a community of scholars and gentlemen. Even though these burdens of position may be undesired or resented, they inhere in the collegiate way of life. If they are disregarded, the effectiveness of the professor and the quality of his college are diminished. The professor owes some of these responsibilities to himself, others to his discipline, his relations with colleagues, and the college administration.

### RESPONSIBILITY TO HIMSELF

The quiet routines of campus life make it easy for the professor to trade his early enthusiasm and vitality for a calm, ponderous, unimaginative, uncreative, and repetitious approach to his teaching. College presidents have remarked that only one in four of their faculty members ever complete any research after their doctoral dissertations. College students comment wryly on the dog-eared and yellowed condition of the professor's ancient lecture notes. These developments are not inevitable. The college teacher is obliged to see that they do not occur. Ortega y Gasset has remarked that there are really only two kinds of people, those who make demands upon themselves and those who do not. The college professor owes it to himself to be self-demanding, alert and questioning in his discipline, concerned about the excellence of his teaching, and optimistic about the influence he can have on the succeeding generations of his students. If he comes to lack faith in himself and interest in his subject, how can he possibly impart either to others?

## RESPONSIBILITY TO HIS DISCIPLINE

The teacher's responsibility to his discipline may be of various kinds. Certainly not every teacher has the competence or the opportunity to make significant and fundamental contributions through new discoveries. Seeking after the truth in his chosen field may be achieved through original and painstaking research, or by a continuing effort to study, evaluate, collate, and interpret in the classroom and in the journals the research of others. Both discovery and dissemination are worthy aspects of the process of research. Responsible scholarship requires the faculty member to be energetic and dedicated in one of these aspects, if he cannot do both. The irresponsible and deplorable attitude is to rest on his doctoral diploma and pretend that the learning of his youth will serve without vigorous cultivation until his retirement.

## RESPONSIBILITY TO HIS COLLEAGUES

"A community of scholars" is the classical definition of a university, and the phrase may serve also to indicate the nature of the professor's responsibility to his colleagues. A college teacher's area of concern and his sphere of influence go beyond his classes, his students, and his department. He is an important part of the college. More than an employee, he is an integral member of the community. As a scholar, he receives benefits from his professional associates, and he owes them reciprocal obligations of cooperation and understanding. These reciprocal obligations include mutual understanding of colleagues, support of their actions when it is possible, and assistance in problems of institutional concern.

A high degree of parochialism is evident on college and university campuses. Although the tables in the faculty club are not reserved by departments, it is cause for speculation if a man from physical education eats with a group from chemistry, or an engineer with the historians. The tendency toward intellectual chauvinism results in misunderstandings of the nature, the purposes, the quality, and the innate human worth of members of other departments. It is difficult to explain the antagonisms among groups of scholars, but impossible to deny their existence. It is also impossible to deny that these hostilities tend to interfere with the effective education of the students. A first responsibility of any faculty member who wishes to join the community of scholars is to understand and evaluate justly the contributions of other departments and other disciplines to the common task of higher education.

A second responsibility to one's colleagues might be defined as a kind of team loyalty. Under the influence of departmental partisanship teachers sometimes criticize and malign other departments or other professors, either in their classrooms or in off-campus conversations. Such behavior is unethical because it is calculated only to cause difficulty and misunderstanding, not to correct deficiencies. The hearers are neither responsible nor competent to adjust the causes of the criticism. Far from disseminating and exaggerating such attitudes, the intelligent and ethical step would be to support and interpret sympathetically other elements of the college community or to maintain a dignified reserve if the evidence does not permit support.

Membership in a university community implies also a measure of responsibility for the life of that community. The college teacher's task is not completed at the end of the class hour. The instructor shares in the burdens of establishing policies and of carrying on the business of his institution. He cannot conscientiously evade participation to some extent in faculty meetings, or service on faculty senates or their committees. These are the channels through which he can contribute to the definition of academic policies, the improvement of educational quality, the conditions of professorial tenure, and the correction of troublesome deficiencies. Committees may sometimes seem to be a sort of cancer in academic life, multiplying endlessly, and consuming inordinate hours of time. Their recent abuse does not vitiate the principle that professional persons should control professional practices; in a college, reasonable participation in committee work is the way professors exercise this control.

### RESPONSIBILITY TO THE ADMINISTRATION

Increasing complexity of college organization and the need for officers to obtain and to protect finances, to plan and maintain buildings, to admit students and to keep their records, and to carry on all of the auxiliary services of a college have resulted in a temporary separation of the teaching function from the administrative function. This is unfortunate. In an earlier day, presidents were faculty members who were sentenced to a brief term of service in handling details so that the other professors could concentrate on teaching. During the middle part of the twentieth century, trustees tended to seek managers rather than scholars to "run" educational institutions; lawyers, generals, politicians, and businessmen were installed as presidents of colleges. Even when a recognized scholar did become president, he was obliged to abandon his scholarship and master a new set of techniques.

A result of this development was a gulf between "management" and "employees" in colleges. Some of the misunderstandings and cross-purposes inherent in this dichotomy are more appropriate to the earliest days of the trade-union movement than to the relations between educators. Both groups, professors and administrators, are dedicated to advancement of the same purposes. Far from being employees in the context of classical economics, the professors are highly competent participants in the enterprise of higher education. They have a responsibility to cooperate, both in attitude toward other workers and through faculty senates, councils, or other formal processes, in the determination of policies and the ratification of decisions. Harmony of operation is not unilateral; but faculties must accept and discharge the responsibility for governance which they have abdicated because of the pressure toward specialization. Increasing involvement of professors (and students) in the selection of department heads, deans, and presidents is a wholesome countertrend. This participation helps the faculty understand the problems of the administrator and tends to diminish the differences in their points of view. In addition, more and more professors direct research institutes or serve as consultants to government and industry, or hold administrative posts in their own colleges for terms of a few years. This democratizing of administration tends to reestablish mutual understanding within the academic community.

## CORRESPONDING RIGHTS

The discussion so far has been pointed at the responsibilities of the college teacher. These responsibilities are complemented by certain rights that are worthy of mention. In return for his cooperation, the college must assure the teacher sufficient *time to teach*, so that he is able to study, to reflect, to prepare, and to evaluate the results of his teaching. Teaching without wisdom is charlatanry; but wisdom does not mature quickly. A second right of the teacher is *freedom to teach*, without external pressures from department, college, or community. If the teacher is willing to discharge his responsibility for wise and informed scholarship, he must not be hindered in its interpretation to his students. *Facilities for teaching* include not only the classroom space, but such essentials as adequate laboratory and library facilities, office space to permit both on-campus study and student conferences, and clerical help to free the scholar from typing, duplicating, and test-scoring duties. *Protection in teaching* is a right that is rarely needed but essential. The professor deserves to know that department heads and all college administrators exist to make his teaching possible and that they will protect him from unnecessary interferences by nonacademic activities as well as from unwarranted attacks from any source— press, parents, or students. Finally, the teacher has a right to *reasonable rewards* for his teaching, in salary, rank, recognition, and in such fringe benefits as retirement, health insurance, travel to professional meetings, and assistance with the costs of publication, if needed.

## RESPONSIBILITIES TO STUDENTS

The self-concepts of professors might provide a basis for a fascinating counterpart to reports on the image of college professors as reported by such authors as Bowen[10] or in a different vein by O'Dowd and Beardsley.[11] No graduate student will have difficulty in identifying several of the stereotype professors: pearls before swine, the "pal" or the "father image," Professor Tweedy, the autocrat of the podium, the cynic, the comic, the high priest of the inner sanctum, and the executive or coordinator. There are indifferent professors, and bored, arrogant, or overworked ones, as well as those who are dull, unprepared, sarcastic, or ingratiating. These are in addition to the majority who are competent and intent. In general, a well-defined and attractive image of the college professor is shared among college students. What are the qualities of personality that make for competence as a professor? Can the teacher's responsibilities to his students be stated positively rather than negatively, and in practical and attainable categories?

A basic and inclusive responsibility of any teacher at any level of schools is *to contribute positively to the intellectual and personal development of his stu-*

[10] Robert Bowen, *The New Professors* (New York: Holt, Rinehart and Winston, Inc., 1960).

[11] Donald D. O'Dowd and David C. Beardsley, "The Image of the College Professor" *A.A.U.P. Bulletin* 47(1961):216-221.

**Figure 2-3.**
A basic and inclusive responsibility of the college teacher is to contribute positively to the intellectual and personal development of his students.

*dents.* As a result of his teaching, students should be changed, even slightly, in several important ways. A first set of changes would result in an extended and increased fund of information and depth of understanding. Obviously, no teacher would maintain his right to foster misunderstanding or falsehood. Second, the teacher will strive to increase the student's ability to use his new knowledge and understanding in solving problems. Third, the instructor will hope to enlarge the student's intellectual curiosity, his sense of satisfaction in worthwhile accomplishment, his confidence in his own powers, his laudable ambitions, his sense of values, and his ideals of citizenship. Finally, the instructor will attempt to develop in students certain of the skills of scholarship in his discipline.

As a part of this broad responsibility to work for the growth of the student, the teacher has a particular responsibility to improve *his own personal and professional competence.* This includes not only thorough knowledge of his discipline, but effective preparation for each class period and a clear, coherent presentation. His lectures should clarify the material and demonstrate relationships, rather than parrot the statements of the textbook. Such competence requires an experimental and evaluative attitude toward teaching and a determination that each successive semester shall show improvement in the quality of his teaching.

## CONDITIONS OF WORK

One of the attractions of the academic life is found in the freedom it offers the instructor to plan his own time; another comes from the several extended periods in the year that are free from stated obligations of classes, office hours, or committee meetings. A competent professor will work as many hours in a year as any other professional person, and just as diligently. His advantage lies in his emancipation, except for the class schedule, from the time clock and the daily routine of eight to five. His work must be done, but much of it can be done away from the office and the classroom and at an hour of his own choosing.

Assigned class hours vary by kinds of institutions and by rank of the faculty member. Few institutions require more than fifteen semester hours of courses from their instructors, and so heavy a load will ordinarily be confined to freshman and sophomore courses. Fifteen units is the most frequent assignment in junior colleges. In four-year colleges and universities, the basic load will more often consist of nine or twelve units, especially for faculty members concerned with graduate instruction and expected to carry on research in addition to their teaching. In a few universities the basic teaching load is as little as six classroom hours a week.

Requirements of this nature are ordinarily stated quite clearly in the staff handbook or other policy statement of a college and can be learned by a new instructor before he accepts a position. The differences in class load are attributable to the autonomy of most colleges and universities, so that each college or at least each system of colleges may establish these policies for itself. The stated purposes of the college, with their relative emphases on teaching and on research, are another factor in determining load. Economic need of the institution is perhaps the controlling influence on class-hour load. The poorer institutions may not be able to afford to increase the size of their faculties to reduce teaching loads and to increase research productivity, whereas universities with more income can use a lighter teaching load as an additional inducement in recruiting talented research professors from less fortunate institutions.

But even in a college dedicated primarily to teaching, the classroom hours are only a part of the total work load of the instructor. A rough estimate of the total work week might be reached by multiplying classroom hours by three or four, depending on the actual situation in a given college. Another generalization suggests that the work week includes fifteen hours of teaching, fifteen hours of preparation, fifteen hours of advising, committee work, and college responsibilities. When college teachers are asked to keep a daily record of their activities during the regular terms, they ordinarily arrive at weekly totals of from fifty to seventy hours of work associated with their teaching assignments.

A simple listing of the usual tasks of the college instructor will serve to indicate why teaching is so time-consuming:

*Planning objectives and activities of the course*—involving conferences with colleagues and support personnel.

*Meeting the classes*, discussion groups, and individual students.

*Preparing for class*—reading, writing notes, checking sources, revising, preparing assignments and syllabi, arranging for charts, maps, demonstration materials, films, projectors, and the like.

*Preparing examinations*, grading, reporting marks.

*Office hours* for student conferences and for advising prospective students and degree candidates.

*Conferences* with colleagues on shared courses, on departmental problems, on development of research proposals or on writing of articles and books; sharpening concepts by discussing them with other specialists.

*Responsibilities to the department, to the college, and to the profession*, which result in academic committee assignments and a number of routine duties for almost every member of the faculty.

*Research*, whether on one's own problems as part of one's conditions of employment, or in keeping in touch with the most recent developments of other scholars in the field.

*Developing orders* for library and laboratory materials.

*Miscellaneous details*—visitors from other campuses, field trips for classes, convocations, correspondence with colleagues or with future or former students, attendance at professional conventions.

*Reading* the current literature. For other workers this activity may be an avocation; for the professor, it is essential if he is to maintain contact with his culture outside of his own special field.

*Taking time for thoughtful discussion* in an unhurried atmosphere with individuals or small groups of faculty or students. This kind of discussion is the essence of the intellectual life and one of the first responsibilities of the professor.

There are many rewarding conditions of work associated with college teaching. Leisure is defined as "freedom or opportunity to do something, the state of having time at one's own disposal." This priceless freedom is afforded to

**Figure 2-4.**
The hope of college teaching based on academic freedom is that, in fair conflict, truth will prevail over error.

comparatively few workers in modern industrialized society and to none more generously than to college teachers. Although leisure is not time to loaf but time to achieve, the college teacher may choose which pressing tasks to defer and which to complete, may plan his work with a minimum of external direction, and is about as free as man may be of supervision and interference.

Other rewards of college teaching are no less important to the teacher, although they are not so tangible as those mentioned. The environment of the campus, with its libraries, cultural events, learned persons, lively young people, and atmosphere of inquiry, is a satisfying and stimulating milieu for the scholar. The opportunity to consort with mature minds and to enlighten and to inspire youthful ones is a challenge to continuous intellectual alertness. The respect of the community is a value not to be dismissed lightly. The freedom to engage in important work and to grow in competence, in depth, in scholarship, and in influence are intangible conditions of the academic life which serve to compensate for the more widely advertised economic disadvantage of the profession.

## ACADEMIC FREEDOM

The college and university can achieve their purposes and contribute effectively to American life only if ideal conditions of academic freedom prevail. If important questions are closed to discussion, if significant problems are taboo for research, if dissenting voices are stilled, or if conformity becomes the price of preferment, the foundations of American civilization are insidiously destroyed. The professor needs the assurance of academic freedom as a safeguard to his self-respect, his scholarly integrity, and his intellectual independence. The institution benefits from a policy of academic freedom because that is its only method of achieving distinction as a source of new knowledge. It is also the most potent attraction for recruiting the ablest and finest for its faculties. The commonwealth, too, has a stake in academic freedom, in spite of the fears and hysteria of pusillanimous pressure groups. In a world of conflict and instability, security must be sought in the deepest understanding and the most widespread diffusion of knowledge. Only by constant questioning can we remain sure that our theories are tenable and that our beliefs are true. Any measure that inhibits the search for deeper understanding and more comprehensive knowledge acts to destroy, not to preserve, civilization.

The essence of academic freedom is the faith that, in fair conflict, truth will prevail over error. In order to protect the right of the scholar to search for truth down any pathway of knowledge and to propound the truth as he sees it in the open forums of his discipline, universities have accepted the principle of academic freedom. It is the principle that the professor will find all doors of inquiry open to him through the provision of time, funds, libraries, and laboratories; that he will be encouraged to pursue knowledge in a creative and idiosyncratic fashion; that he will be urged to publish his findings in his classrooms and in the journals; and that he will be protected from reprisal for unpopular points of view or for controversial discoveries. Only under these conditions can knowledge advance and society prosper.

In the twentieth century, earlier centers of irritation have become accepted and even fashionable. Ideas in psychiatry, biology, astronomy, or physics that once caused historic controversy and persecution are now accepted routinely by even the least intellectual and most conservative groups of citizens. No professor has been in danger recently because of his theories of cosmic space or his interpretation of the causes of disease. Recent confrontations have concerned questions of politics, economics, and faculty participation in determining policy for their institutions. The rise of student activism in protest against the draft and against racism has been accompanied on several campuses by faculty militancy and even strikes demanding changes in conditions of work and salary increases. In reaction, trustees and some lay groups have voiced threats of punitive action to curb free speech on campus. The ostensible causes change with the times, but the recurrent issue remains the desire of some powerful elements of society to curb the freedom of the academic world to exercise constitutionally guaranteed rights. The scholar, on the other hand, insists upon his right and that of his opponents to express and to discuss responsibly any issue, any unpopular point of view. Intellectual controversy and discussion are the primary paths to wisdom. No principle of immunity protects the ideas of the professor from attack; but his freedom to express them must be held inviolate.

The major safeguard of academic freedom to consider controversial problems is academic tenure, designed to guarantee the scholar against loss of his livelihood because of new and unpalatable ideas. Not all colleges and universities observe tenure provisions, although their adoption is spreading. In public institutions, academic tenure rights may be guaranteed by law; in private colleges, their status rests upon action by the board of trustees. In general, tenure involves a vested right in his position for a teacher after a stated period of probationary service; ordinarily provision is made for retirement at a stated age, for the dismissal for cause of the tenure teacher, and for his protection against arbitrary and punitive discrimination in matters of salary, duties, or rank.

It is only natural that controversial questions should arise concerning the observance or the suspension of a teacher's tenure rights. Granted that incompetence should be a just cause for dismissal, how can one be sure that incompetence and not dislike is the true cause of a given dismissal? How can incompetence be measured? Along with his right of freedom in the search for truth, the professor assumes a responsibility not to teach what he knows to be false; but how can college presidents judge these matters? Tenure is also attacked because it provides blanket protection for the mediocre as well as for the able professor. Critics suggest that it should be easier to discharge an unwanted teacher. But in a community of scholars this difficulty of dismissal is precisely the strength of tenure provisions. The unwanted teacher will often be not the incompetent teacher but the effective, the exciting, or the unconventional teacher. Society can afford the cost of protecting a small percentage of lazy, inefficient, and unworthy professors so that it may protect itself from the loss of its critics and its frontier thinkers, whose function in a free society is utterly essential.

A strong force in the protection of the rights of college teachers has been Committee A on Academic Freedom and Tenure of the American Association of University Professors. When apparent violations of the principles of academic freedom and tenure endorsed by the Association and several other associations and societies are reported to Committee A, it makes a preliminary investigation. Often this first inquiry leads to adjustment of the controversy, or establishes the fact that no infringement did occur. If it seems after full investigation that the principles have been violated, the A.A.U.P. may vote to censure the offending college administration, as a warning to professors considering employment at the censured college and as a quasi-persuasion for the administration to revise its procedures. Censure is considered to be not so much a punitive measure as a means toward the reestablishment of conditions that will enable faculty members to fulfill their obligations to themselves and to a democratic and academic community.

The new professor should accept the obligations as well as the protections of academic freedom. He should be zealous in protecting it for his colleagues and equally zealous in making certain that he himself is worthy of it. For academic freedom without academic responsibility would be a fraud, destined to early decay.

## THE INSTRUCTOR AND PROFESSIONAL SOCIETIES

Professional organizations and public agencies perform important services to the college teacher. There are two major categories of organizations that are of interest to every college teacher. Within each category are so many separate associations that no professor could afford to belong to all of the appropriate ones. On the other hand, every professor ought to feel obligated to associate himself with his colleagues in at least one group within each category. Some of the societies are concerned with problems common to all faculty members and all departments in higher education. The other organizations limit themselves either to a broad curricular field or to a single discipline. Both kinds publish bulletins or journals of interest to their members.

A governmental agency of service to teachers in colleges as well as to administrators and to state boards is the Division of Higher Education, U.S. Office of Education, Department of Health, Education, and Welfare. This division compiles statistics of higher education, prepares a directory of colleges and universities, and issues a monthly bulletin entitled *Higher Education*. It is also responsible for the administration of several of the Federal programs of appropriation for higher education institutions, such as the Education Professions Development Act of 1967.

An association of interest to college teachers from all disciplines is the American Association of University Professors. Its quarterly *Bulletin* reports on matters of academic freedom, economic status, and other professional concerns, and includes articles of general interest about college teachers and college teaching.

The American Association for Higher Education is an independent organization associated with the National Education Association. Membership in the Association is open to all classes of academic workers, joining administrators and faculty members in harmonious consideration of common problems; it has frequently represented the viewpoint of higher education at Congressional hearings. It holds an annual meeting in early March and prepares the useful and significant annual report, *Current Issues in Higher Education*. Its leaflet, *College and University Bulletin*, is issued semimonthly during the academic year and includes notes of important events and occasional special articles. It has also sponsored the preparation and commercial publication of several important books on college teaching, college counseling, and general education.

The American Federation of Teachers limits its membership to teaching faculty members only. As a union affiliated with the American Federation of Labor, it is concerned primarily with economic issues for teachers at all levels of education. It considers collective bargaining to be basically an adversary relationship, and has not hesitated to invoke strike sanctions in public schools and in colleges in pursuit of improved salaries and improved conditions of work for teachers and of educational opportunity for students.

The American Junior College Association consists primarily of institutional members, although individual memberships are welcomed. It conducts annual meetings, prepares the annual *Junior College Directory*, and gathers material for the quadrennial reference book, *American Junior Colleges*. Its periodical, *Junior College Journal*, carries articles of interest to teachers in the subject areas as well as to administrators of junior colleges.

Special interest associations for college teachers, too numerous to list in this chapter, provide useful services for their memberships. The annual meetings provide opportunities to renew acquaintances and to hear and present papers on recent research; they serve as academic marketplaces for those in search of new positions and new teachers; and their bulletins serve as outlets for reports of studies, discussions of new viewpoints, and book reviews to keep the professor in touch with developments in his discipline.

## THE INSTRUCTOR IN SEARCH OF A POSITION

An older and more leisurely tradition that the scholar must never seem to want and under no circumstances ask for a position is weakening under the pressure of rising needs for teachers. Except in a few highly desirable institutions, a direct application is no longer a guarantee that the applicant will *not* be employed. Rapidly growing colleges do not hesitate to send a personnel officer to university campuses to interview and employ, even to proselyte, new members for their faculties. University placement offices also are now playing more active roles in college employment. Nevertheless, personal recommendations are still the most usual method by which newly graduated doctors first come to the attention of deans or department heads who are in search of teachers.

Preliminary correspondence about a position may often proceed as far as careful consideration of a candidate's suitability, and even so far as a decision to offer him the position, before the candidate hears of it. When a dean and a departmental faculty have decided that they need, in a new position or as a replacement, an assistant professor with certain competencies, letters are addressed to trusted colleagues in graduate schools, asking for recommendations. After all recommendations have been screened, university placement offices will be asked to send their files on two or three of the most desired nominees. Opportunities will then be arranged for an interview, or at least for some fairly searching correspondence, with the available nominee who is chosen. The entire process seems to disregard the stake of the graduate student in his own future, but there are several steps that he can take in order to increase his chances of suitable recommendation.

First, of course, he must become known to the department head and to influential professors in his own department. The best way to achieve this aim is by thorough, conscientious, and able performance in study. Outstanding papers, laboratory work, and seminar presentations will inevitably be noticed by professors and cause interest in the future plans of the student who presents them. Beyond this, the graduate student would do well to identify himself with his graduate department as much as possible. It is a mistake for the married and/or employed graduate student to come to the campus only when he is required to be there. Social contacts and counseling conferences with members of the departmental faculty will enable them to know of the candidate's personality, home situation, ambitions, and potentialities. Sometimes favorable opportunities may arise for the graduate assistant to teach one or two classes on a topic in which he is especially competent. Although an overeager graduate student can become a nuisance in cultivating his professors, even this might be more rewarding than knowing his instructors only in the classroom. They cannot recommend a student who is merely a name on an examination paper.

A further important step is for the graduate student to register with the placement service of his university, which often receives the first notice of a desirable teaching vacancy. The director of the service will usually check first with the department, but he may be able to suggest names to the department head from those listed in his files. The convenience to prospective employers, however, may be more important than the advantage to the student. Placement office files gather academic records, personal history, and letters of recommendation about a candidate in one convenient dossier, so that the qualities of the several candidates can be compared with ease. Employing deans are likely to prefer such a folder to a miscellany of original papers submitted by a candidate. This preference becomes a requirement if the dean wishes to complete some preliminary screening of nominees before he raises the hopes of the two or three he wishes to interview. Finally, a professor recommending the candidate can write one careful letter that will serve as a number of nominations for him, instead of separate personal letters each time the student is considered for a different position.

Personal letters of application are becoming more acceptable as initial contacts of prospective instructors with college officers. Several precautions should be observed in their use. Each letter should be an original, not a ditto or mimeographed circular. It should be addressed to a person, with his correct name and title, rather than to "The President" or "Dean of Arts College." The letter should indicate subtly that the writer has some knowledge of the institution other than its name, that he is attracted by elements of its curriculum, by its location, by friends who have described it, or even as a result of a thorough study of its catalog. Such a letter may be accompanied by a duplicate sheet giving basic biographical facts, such as age, educational background, family status, work and military experience, academic honors, publications, and college activities. With this information, a dean can decide whether he wishes to investigate the application further or whether he will not have any suitable vacancy that year.

The annual meetings of learned societies serve as recruiting grounds for faculty members. The graduate student who can afford to attend the meetings of his own association will be stimulated by the papers presented and excited by the opportunity to meet and talk with the great names in the field, whose texts he has studied and whose research he has followed. At the same time, many of these leaders are looking over the new crop of doctorates in search of likely candidates for future appointment. The advertising world has introduced the concept of "visibility" to express the degree of notice that must be attracted to a product before it can be marketed successfully. In a period of increasing supply of college teachers, the well-prepared graduate student can increase his chances of being offered the most appropriate position by ethical and tasteful efforts to increase his "visibility."

## SUMMARY

The social importance of the college professor is growing as enrollments increase and as the economy needs more and more educated personnel. Nevertheless, the basic obligations of the professor continue—to pursue and disseminate knowledge to the limit of his powers. The position is one of unlimited intangible rewards and of steadily improving real rewards. Certainly, as an occupation, being a professor compares favorably in status, both real and superficial, with other kinds of employment open to the scholarly person.

## RELATED READING

American Association for Higher Education. *Faculty Participation in Academic Governance.* Washington: The Association, 1967.

American Association for Higher Education. *Current Issues in Higher Education.* San Francisco: Jossey-Bass, Inc. (annually, with varying sub-titles).

American Association of University Professors. *A.A.U.P. Bulletin* (quarterly).

American Junior College Association. *The Junior College Journal* (monthly).

Brown, David G. *The Mobile Professors.* Washington: American Council on Education, 1969.

Estrin, Herman A., and Delmer W. Goode. *College and University Teaching.* Dubuque: William C. Brown Company, 1964.

Gross, Edward, and Paul V. Grambsch. *University Goals and Academic Power.* Washington: American Council on Education, 1968.

Hefferlin, J.B. Lon. *Dynamics of Academic Reform.* San Francisco: Jossey-Bass, Inc., 1969.

Hutchins, Robert M. *The Learning Society.* New York: Frederick A. Praeger, Inc., 1968.

*Improving College and University Teaching* (quarterly). 101 Waldo Hall, Oregon State University, Corvallis, 97331.

Lee, Calvin B. T. (ed.). *Improving College Teaching.* Washington: American Council on Education, 1967.

McKeachie, Wilbert J. *Teaching Tips* (sixth edition). Lexington, Mass.: D. C. Heath and Co., 1969.

Mayhew, Lewis B. *Graduate and Professional Education, 1980.* New York: McGraw-Hill Book Company, 1970.

Metzger, W. P., et al. *Dimensions of Academic Freedom.* Urbana: University of Illinois Press, 1969.

# chapter three /
# A SYSTEMATIC
# APPROACH TO
# COLLEGE TEACHING /

THE INSTRUCTIONAL SYSTEM • INSTRUCTIONAL OBJEC-
TIVES • STUDENTS IN THE INSTRUCTIONAL SYSTEM
• PROFESSORS AND OTHER SPECIALISTS • NON-HUMAN
RESOURCES FOR INSTRUCTION • LOGISTIC CAPABILITY
• EVALUATION AND FEEDBACK • SUMMARY • RELATED
READING

The humanist is likely to consider systems analysis to be a tool of value only in commercial and industrial enterprises, and to dismiss it as inappropriate to the solution of problems relating to his own planning of classroom activities. But his distrust of this alien procedure is unfortunate. Application of logical examination to instructional problems, inherently a part of the systems approach, might very well result in more effective presentation of the informational content of any course. Even more important, however, is the fact that efficiency in information-presenting resulting from this process might free the instructor to accomplish more of the interpersonal, interpretive, and intuitive tasks of teaching.

## THE INSTRUCTIONAL SYSTEM

The concept of the instructional process as a system that can be analyzed is basically quite simple. The system begins with a set of ends to be accomplished by instructional efforts (or operations) of the members of the system. These ends have been called by various names—goals, objectives, aims. In essence, objectives describe changes that are expected to develop in the behavior of students as a result of the instruction they experience.

### SYSTEM ELEMENTS

If accepted ends are to be achieved, a variety of activities must be engaged in by persons of various talents, using materials and equipment that are available and appropriate to the task. The simplest possible instructional system, of course, is the one that consists of "Mark Hopkins on one end of a log and one student on the other end." In increasing the complexity of the system, these two elements (teacher and student) are supplemented by books, writing materials, classrooms, examinations oral and written, projectors, tapes, television cameras, computers, admissions offices and registrars, and towering echelons of college administrators.

The systems approach to instructional planning seeks to understand and evaluate the contribution of each of the components of the system to achievement of its stated goals, so that the optimum combination of elements may be chosen for utilization in instruction. In more formal terms, an instructional system may be defined as an assemblage of interrelated elements (faculty, students, buildings, materials, equipment) that operates in an organized manner to prepare and present instructional messages by means of the distribution, interpretation, refinement, and application of information. The system, to be effective, must include elements sensitive to feedback and capable of evaluation and adjustment.

In no sense does the systems approach diminish the importance of the instructor. Rather, it identifies those portions of instruction that require the expert intervention of the scholar; by effective and imaginative utilization of other elements in the system (including the student himself) it frees the instructor to apply his expertise. An analogy of this situation may be found in the application of technology to medicine. Whereas the physician of half a century ago was at once diagnostician, surgeon, pharmacist, nurse, X-ray technologist, and laboratory technician, he now delegates many routine tasks to persons of less demanding training. He may even delegate to them the operation of several items of electronic equipment, such as the electrocardiograph. Thus, he not only receives more accurate information, but is also freed to apply his own skills to interpreting diagnostic information and to prescribing necessary treatment. A wholehearted adoption in education of the systematic approach would permit the same economical use of the rare talents of the instructor, as well as the talents of each of the other human and material components of the system.

## A SYSTEMATIC TEACHING APPROACH

A rational development of the systems approach requires recognition of the very real distinction between teaching and educational information-giving. Both of these instructional functions are essential, but they are certainly not the same. Informing may usually be performed quite adequately and economically through planned use of books, records and tapes, films, or computers. Most often, however, teaching requires the person-to-person or person-to-group contribution of the instructor as motivator and assigner, questioner, clarifier, illuminator, evaluator, and director of the intellectual exchange that leads to learning. The systems approach is an avenue to introducing this separation of duties and a means of emphasizing that it will not occur as the result of chance or enthusiasm alone, but only as a carefully planned and anticipated outcome of the process.

The necessary elements to be considered in any systematic approach to instruction may be grouped under six principal headings:

(1) Instructional purposes, stated as intended changes in the behavior of students
(2) the initial status, capabilities, and purposes of the students
(3) the status and capabilities of the professors and corollary professional and technical staff
(4) the status and capabilities of certain nonhuman resources of the educational institution
(5) techniques of managing the availability of each of the elements of the system—logistic capability
(6) program evaluation and improvement.

## INSTRUCTIONAL OBJECTIVES

Clear and forthright expression of precise and measurable outcomes of instruction is the first and perhaps the most difficult part of the systematic approach to higher education. Professors often object to the rigorous examination of their

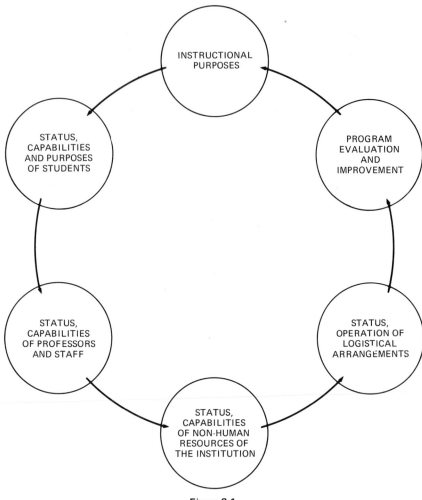

**Figure 3-1.**
A systematic approach to college teaching.

own purposes on the grounds that student intellectual growth is intangible and can be measured only after years have passed. Besides, they argue, any good teacher knows intuitively what it is he is trying to accomplish; teaching is an art, and it will wither if subjected to close examination. Yet it is undeniable that, if objectives are so esoteric and immaterial that their attainment by students cannot be measured, then the instructor can never be sure that he has achieved anything.

Educational objectives, essential to the planning of educational processes and to the evaluation of the outcomes of instruction, have been defined by Bloom as:

> ... explicit formulations of the ways in which students are expected to be changed by the educative process. That is, the ways in which they will change in their thinking, their feelings, and their actions. ... The formulation of educational objectives is a matter of conscious choice on the part of the teaching staff, based on previous experience and aided by consideration of several kinds of data. ... It should be clear that objectives are not only the goals toward which the curriculum is shaped and toward which instruction is guided, but they are also the goals that provide the detailed specification for the construction and use of evaluative techniques.[1]

If objectives are to serve as the basis for systematic planning of instruction and evaluation, they must reach beyond the level of appreciation, understanding, enjoyment, realization, or similar abstractions. The objectives for a course must add specific behaviors to such broad qualitative expectations of the teacher. A task description that requires the student "to write an English sonnet with correct use of meter and rhyme scheme, and consisting of three quatrains and a couplet" is more precise and more measurable than "to understand and appreciate Elizabethan poetry." Similarly measurable goals include "to be able to solve within fifteen minutes ..." or "to recognize in a list of disparate items ..."

In his programmed monograph *Preparing Instructional Objectives*, Mager suggests four qualities of meaningful objectives.[2] First, he says, an objective must be stated in clear unambiguous terms, so that the student or another instructor can understand precisely what is expected. Such statements as "to appreciate Bach" or "to understand the causes of World War II" are susceptible to many different interpretations. Moreover, it is not at all clear to the reader how the appreciation or the understanding will be demonstrated. The worthwhile objectives suggested must be expanded by a statement of the behavior of the student that will demonstrate that he has reached the objective. If in fact it proves impossible to indicate any overt behavior that will accompany the

---

[1] Benjamin S. Bloom (ed.), *Taxonomy of Educational Objectives: The Classification of Educational Goals. Handbook I: Cognitive Domain.* (New York: David McKay Company, Inc., 1956), pp. 26-27.

[2] Robert F. Mager, *Preparing Instructional Objectives* (Palo Alto, Calif.: Fearon Publishers, 1962), pp. 10-53.

realization of the objective by the student, perhaps it would be well to restate the objective more modestly and concretely, so that both the instructor and the student are fully aware of what is expected of the student. The outcomes of learning are not solely metaphysical or transcendental.

Mager's second quality requires that the objective identify the "terminal behavior." When he has succeeded in learning the material or the skill required, what will he be able to do to demonstrate his success? Write something? Identify items within a class of items? Construct or cook or produce something? Recite? Discuss the writings of an author so that listeners may decide whether or not to read the works for themselves? At this point, the objective "to understand the causes of World War II" may be rewritten "to demonstrate an awareness of the complexity of causation of World War II by listing three explanations (or any number) derived from writers on each side of the conflict." Both the student and a substitute instructor or a reader would understand from such a statement what the student was expected to do in this case.

Further specificity in the objective can be provided through the third quality suggested by Mager: under what conditions will the behavior be demonstrated? In the objective cited, may the student use the course textbook while writing his answer? Will he be in a proctored examination room, without notes or reference materials? May he write his paper at home or in the library? How much time will be allowed him? The conditions of performance include time limits, types of materials provided (books, chemicals, tape recorded stimuli, statistical tables, or lists of items from which the student is to select as directed by the objective).

The fourth of Mager's qualities of a meaningful objective is that it must state the criterion of success—the number of items right, or the permissible margin of error (as in typing), or the speed of accomplishment of an assigned task. A meaningful and communicating objective, then:

(1)  is stated in concrete and unambiguous terms
(2)  defines the behavior expected of the successful student
(3)  outlines the conditions under which the behavior will be demonstrated
(4)  describes the criteria of success in achieving the objective.

From this discussion, it is apparent that there is a considerable similarity between the concepts of instructional objectives and examination questions. If student and instructor accept at the outset of a term certain objectives of their joint efforts in a subject, they will be able to demonstrate at the outset by means of a pretest where the student scores at the beginning of the term, and to measure at the end how far he has progressed. The initial goal and the final test are inseparable: the purpose of objectives is to define the expected changes in student behavior as a result of the activities of the course; the purpose of final examinations is to demonstrate for teacher and for student whether and to what extent those changes have in fact occurred.

Because of this connection between the statement of the objective and the evaluation of its attainment, a clear and complete statement of objectives must be the first step in a systematic analysis of instruction. Important objectives are difficult to state, but it is imperative that the effort be made.

## STUDENTS IN THE INSTRUCTIONAL SYSTEM

A great deal of college teaching has been carried on in the troubadour mode: "I want you to know about this; I will tell you about this in an interesting way; then you will know it." In the middle ages, when few people read, when there was little organized knowledge, and when listening was the prime mode of learning, this technique sometimes succeeded. In the age of electronic media, however, constant high-decibel noise has taught the young not to listen. It is more true in the 1970s than ever before that if a student does not participate actively in his education he will not learn. Talk is worse than passively "not enough;" too often even the best of talk is simply a crashing bore.

The upshot of these developments is, in the words of John M. Culkin, that communication "consists not in saying things but in having things heard. . . . The school may decide that history is *important for* the student, but the role of the teacher is to make history relevant to the student . . . . The teacher has to be constantly engaged in audience research."[3] In the frame of reference of the present chapter, Culkin's observation may be interpreted as implying that the systematic approach involves thinking about all aspects of the teaching-learning sequence, especially about the learner, rather than concentrating solely on the instructor's purposes and activities.

The most obvious quality of students that is of concern to the instructor is their beginning status. What is the intellectual level of the class? How much of

[3]John M. Culkin, S.J., "A Schoolman's Guide to Marshall McLuhan," *Saturday Review,* March 18, 1967, pp. 51-53, 70-72. Italics in original.

the subject do they know already? What learning experiences and attitudes toward instruction have they brought with them from their previous schooling? Why did they enroll in this course, of all the possible offerings of the university? What is their general level of motivation, and to what extent can it be heightened by any kind of activity within the total system that is the course? Some answers to such questions can be learned from the results of a pretest, and used as guides for assignments both for those who already know most of what the instructor planned to teach, and for those who fall far short of his early optimistic assumptions. In addition, some answers can be postulated from previous knowledge of the characteristics of the entire college generation.

## DIFFERENCES IN INTELLECTUAL ABILITY

Admissions policies of most colleges and universities permit enrollment of students who vary widely in intellectual ability and aptitude for success in higher education. It is not uncommon, in typical freshmen classes, for IQs to range from 105 to 150. While there is always a range of IQs in any class, it will be pitched at higher or lower levels in some classes than in others, for one or more reasons. Some honors program classes, for example, are restricted to high-ability students; upper division classes will tend to have in them students who have managed to survive two or more years at college and who have demonstrated aptitude for meeting its academic demands; and students enrolled in some notably tough courses will frequently be those whose academic records have been good and who have had preliminary success in the field.

It is a valuable procedure for the instructor to ascertain the distribution and range of intellectual abilities in his classes. He will be able to use this knowledge in several significant ways: (1) to decide the optimum point at which to pitch the initial instruction of the course, (2) to compare achievement in different sections of the same course, (3) to settle upon realistic performance and grading standards, (4) to guard against spending too much time, perhaps unwittingly, teaching either the bright or the not so bright in the same section, and (5) to suggest needs and ways to individualize instruction for students of varying ability.

## DIFFERENCES IN EXPERIENCE

Differences of several kinds will be noted in the experience backgrounds of any group of college students. In the same class, for example, there may be both freshmen and seniors whose acquaintance with college traditions, study techniques, or generally useful college know-how will vary considerably. And, unless rigid prerequisites are enforced, students who are well grounded in the discipline of the course may be enrolled along with some making their first contact with it.

Differences in experience may stem also from the varieties and amounts of work in which students have engaged, of travels they have completed, or of significant cultural experiences to which they have been exposed. Still other differences may be closely related to their advantaged or disadvantaged cultural or economic backgrounds.

The instructor who notes these differences is often able to use the information in assessing the adequacy of academic performances, in making adaptations to fit course activities and course requirements to the clientele he serves, or in drawing upon student experiences to illumine his course.

### DIFFERENCES IN REACTIONS TO LEARNING EXPERIENCES

Research and experience show clearly that there are differences in student ability to profit from learning experiences presented orally, in print, in a manner employing audiovisual technology, or through a variety of other media. Some students appear to be able to grasp the thread of historical continuity, for example, when lecture statements are accompanied by chalkboard time lines or relationship charts; others find these aids unnecessary or, in some instances, actual handicaps to comprehension.

A part of this difference in the ability of students to profit from certain learning activities may be traced to their previous experience and practice. Another may be attributed to personality factors, such as shyness or self-assurance, made evident in discussion sections. Various physical factors may also be important. Students with low energy levels or with generally poor health will be handicapped in keeping up with assignments. Numerous college students who do not read with sufficient speed and comprehension must work harder or longer than normal to complete their studies. Others, though they are capable of reading well, do their assignments inefficiently because they fail to make effective use of the library.

Instructors who are aware of the presence of handicaps among the total college population will look for them among their own students. They will be able to adjust learning activities, as feasible and desirable, and to help students become more skilled as learners. They may use a variety of instructional

**Figure 3-2.**
It is known that students profit differently from learning activities presented orally, in print, through technological means, or as "hands on" experience.

materials and methods in a conscious effort to permit all students to participate maximally rather than to limit participation to those possessing certain communication skills. Without in any way compromising the integrity of instruction, instructors may also individualize assignments and encourage students with well-developed skills to use them. They may make particular efforts to help students learn how to study more effectively and to make fuller and better use of the library. Finally, by analyzing student reports, term papers, and results of interviews they may obtain data needed to decide whether to refer certain students to college personnel counselors, to reading or writing clinics, or to the health office.

## DIFFERENCES IN REASONS FOR ENROLLING

It might seem reasonable to expect that most registrants in one's course are there because they are interested in the subject. But it is more realistic to recognize that, for at least a few persons, the course may only represent a hurdle requirement between them and some important goal—such as graduation. It is remotely possible, too, that others may regard it as a snap course calculated to raise a dangerously low grade-point average. Still others may register because it is offered at a time that allows them to fill out a class schedule in conformity with outside work assignments or other obligations. Perhaps the majority of the students are there because the course represents a reasonable means of fulfilling major, minor, or general education requirements. But to assume initially high interest in the course even by these students would probably be unwise.

In any event, the instructor will usually find it interesting to hypothesize as to why students enroll in his classes. While he may make certain deductions as a result of student performances, interviews, or reactions to questionnaires, he will recognize that there are often differences between what students say and their actual reasons. Judgments based on informed guesses should therefore be tentative and subject to change as the course progresses. But by knowing that differences in interest do exist, the instructor may make several important adaptations in his course. Carefully developed assignments and requirements, for example, can do much to dispel the mistaken notion that the course is a snap, and students whose initial interest is low or neutral may be stimulated to see its purpose and utility.

## DIFFERENCES IN MOTIVATION

Learners differ not only in their reasons for enrolling in a course, but also in their motivations to fulfill its learning requirements. It is well known, for example, that grades motivate most students, but not in the same way or to the same extent. Demonstrated application of the subject matter to mutually accepted purposes of teacher and students is a better motivation than fear of failure.

In general, an instructor who is informed about the characteristics of his students is better able to present the materials of his course in meaningful ways. Computerized admission and registration procedures can provide interested instructors with pertinent information about their classes. Instructors who use computer instructional programs in their teaching can be supplied with daily progress reports on the learning of each student. The systematic approach recognizes that increased understanding of the learner is an important step toward improved instruction.

## PROFESSORS AND OTHER SPECIALISTS

The concept of the classroom teacher is obsolescent in the lower schools as well as in the colleges. It has been rendered passé by the geometric increase in the amount of knowledge, by the growth of enrollments, by the introduction of varied and effective media of communicating knowledge, and quite simply by the realization that there are better ways to utilize the talents of the scholar than repetitive information giving.

Instead of expecting each member of the faculty to be a general practitioner, the college of the future will recognize that individual differences in aptitude apply to professors as well as to students. Systematic utilization of diverse talents promises to improve both the challenge of teaching and the quality of educational opportunity for students. Instructional teams—perhaps not all members of the team will be on the same campus—will contribute specialized abilities to the teaching task. Some will serve as *presenters* or lecturers or interpreters, imparting the personal spark that is too apt to be missing from even the best mediated presentation. It is possible that this presenter may not even be a research scholar, but rather a scholar-teacher who is well informed and widely read in his field. The instructor will no longer be absolute monarch in his private bailiwick, free to ramble as he wills, secure in the knowledge that his future depends more on his published works and the personal impressions of his senior colleagues than on his reputation and achievement with students. Instead, he will be a cooperating member of a group that includes a subject analyst, a learning diagnostician, discussion leaders and tutors, and supporting technical and logistic staff. In a good many courses, the same person may bear several of the roles to be described; but he will recognize that the interrelated tasks differ in nature, and that he is perhaps less competent in some of them than in others.

The *subject-analyst* will be concerned with a number of preliminaries to instructional communication. He will be able to state clearly the basic concepts and the structure of the discipline, and to derive from these the goals of instruction in this course and their relation to the goals of antecedent and subsequent courses. He will be aware of the value of variety in classroom procedures, and be able to suggest in the overall plan of the course those techniques that promise to be effective in moving students toward the achievement of the goals. He will suggest assignments for student participation that will avoid busywork and concentrate instead on relevance of the task to the goals of both the instructional team and the learners. As a part of his planning assignment, he will establish evaluation or feedback activities so that both professor and students may be informed of the degrees of their success in their respective roles.

A *diagnostician* member of the instructional team will serve a vital function in adapting course requirements to the learning needs of individual students. By means of conferences, written examinations, computer-presented exercises, reports of discussion leaders, and analysis of student products, the diagnostician will seek to determine the progress of each student, and to prescribe activities that will encourage the brightest student to grow in the breadth of his knowledge and the depth of his insights, and also to permit the least able student to achieve objectives of the course at minimally acceptable levels.

*Discussion leaders and tutors* will be needed in the system in order to restore the face-to-face contact of students and faculty that have been lost in many of the large-class schedules of the recent past, and that are so important a difference in the distinction between information-giving and teaching. Discussion leaders will need scholarship in the field of the course at least at the post-baccalaureate level. Moreover, they must be sufficiently free of their own graduate study demands that they can become thoroughly acquainted with the goals, the methods, and the expectations of the total instructional team. They must be an integral part of that team, and participate in the planning and presentation of the materials of the course. It is probably utopian to hope that the post of discussion leader might command such prestige and recognition that it could qualify as a worthy continuing academic career goal.

*Supporting staff* are integral and essential parts of the systematic approach to instruction. If the goal is competent and sophisticated analysis and performance of instruction, the need for specialized talents is evident. The scholar-teacher must be assisted in his endeavors to keep fully abreast of research in his discipline, and assisted in selecting from the annual flood of new writing those articles that are appropriate for his course and his students. Graphic technicians are needed to prepare charts and transparencies and visualizations of all kinds for use in connection with available and appropriate modes of presentation—TV, 8mm films, audio-tapes, large transparencies, or bulletin boards. Computer programmers and electronic technicians may also be needed, especially if large-group presentation and independent study are to be parts of the system. Finally, the need for stenographic assistance must be emphasized as a part of the instructional team. Far too many clerical tasks are performed at present on far too many campuses by the most highly educated and expensive members of the faculty.

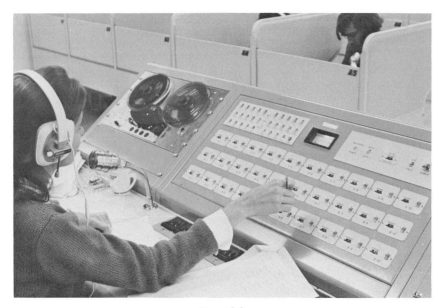

**Figure 3-3.**
New specialized skills are required of those who teach in the modern language laboratory.

The *team leader* is the key to the success of the entire effort. In specialized courses and on small campuses he may be the entire team, or he may share certain of the support personnel with other departments or even with the entire faculty. Nevertheless, in even the most simple instructional system he is the one who must coordinate all of the activities, who will exemplify the new definition of the professor as the planner, motivator of students, presenter and clarifier of information not otherwise economically available, and the user, not the servant, of technology. He must be the one who restores relevance and humanism to the campus, by imaginative and enthusiastic emulation of professionals in other fields (medicine, engineering, law, or business) who improve their effectiveness and their income through specialization of activity.

## NONHUMAN RESOURCES FOR INSTRUCTION

A fourth element in the instructional system consists of the status and capabilities of the nonhuman resources of the institution. In consideration of the initial objectives of the system, are the library collections, audiovisual equipment and materials, television capabilities, and computer installations sufficiently rich and suitably administered and controlled so that they may contribute effectively to the achievement of the instructional purposes? Which functions of the system may be performed best (or most economically) by:

*instruments alone*—mechanical, electronic, electrical—in some of which materials (films, cassette tape recordings, videotapes, slides, or others) are used;
*non-technical materials alone*—(books, programmed materials, syllabi, assignment sheets);
*human beings*—instructors and students, alone or in appropriate combinations with other persons, instruments, or media.

Such analysis of functions should provide clues as to ways of insuring the optimum utilization of the human and non-human resources available to the system. The analysis should also emphasize that some, but not all, learning experiences require the intervention of the instructor.

Applications of nonhuman resources to the instructional system have implications far beyond the usual classroom. Budgetary considerations are among the most pressing of these. Are additional funds justified and available for the particular system? Are physical facilities—specialized classrooms, carrels, large-group installations, small-group discussion rooms, and the like—available or possible? Are the institution's administrative policies and regulations adaptable to the system? Are there spaces to permit independent study by students? Problems and applications of resources are discussed in greater detail in Chapter Five.

## LOGISTIC CAPABILITY

Any teacher who has ordered a film for class use that was not available until weeks after he had planned to show it will appreciate the importance of logistics in the instructional system. The entire process starts in the institutional office of academic planning, in which decisions are made that encourage or discourage the assignment of funds to innovative and systematic approaches to instruction. Institutional and departmental plans adopted at the appropriate levels of the college are given fiscal reality and recognition in the programmed budget, a process by which priorities are assigned to the elements of the institutional plan, and funds appropriated to support the activities that have been agreed on.

At the level of the subsystem, the course planner, it is likely that existing logistic capability must be accepted as it has been developed prior to the immediate need of the instructional team. The elements of instructional logistics are support personnel, material resources, and arrangements for the ready availability of these when and where they are needed. Planning requires a realistic knowledge of the total logistic capability of the institution.

The authors have observed that *support personnel*, when they are available at all in a college or university, are eager to contribute unstintingly to the improvement of instruction. The great problem seems to be the shortage of competent personnel and of time to meet all of the demands for their services. An early task for the instructor who endeavors to plan his course thoroughly and systematically, making full use of appropriate resources of the institution, is to become acquainted with the support personnel in the office of instructional resources. In a fully staffed office, he can expect to find planning personnel who understand his discipline; programmers who are versed in the techniques of stating objectives and of developing step-by-step instructional sequences for independent study; artists and photographers to assist in designing and in producing visual aids; and technicians who can operate equipment and keep it in running order.

In addition to the support personnel, he will find inventories of the sorts of *equipment* that are on hand or obtainable, ranging from overhead projectors and slide and film projectors to tape recorders and videotape equipment, together with a library of films and tapes for use with them. It may well be that the available equipment includes one or more items of which the instructor is only vaguely aware, but that will solve some problem of presentation that has previously been difficult for him.

The analysis of the logistics of the learning resources center will include consideration of *arrangements to distribute technological equipment* that must be physically present in the classroom, as well as to disseminate sound or images through cable systems to campus classrooms or auditoriums. In general, the more convenient it is for the instructor to assemble equipment and students (in groups or individually) in the appropriate place at the proper time, the more likely he is to make use of instructional techniques other than his own voice. Contemporary attempts to solve some of the problems of availability of equipment and materials include the construction of specially equipped lecture rooms, closed-circuit TV between buildings, the assignment of an assortment of equipment to departments for easy checkout by instructors, and permanent installation of projection and sound equipment in many or even in all classrooms of new buildings. These applications are discussed in detail in Chapter Five.

## EVALUATION AND FEEDBACK

Paradoxically, the first and the last steps in the systematic approach to instruction involve evaluation and feedback. At the initial stage of analysis behavioral objectives specify what students ought to be able to do after they have completed the activities of the course. During the instructional period, and more formally at its end, close analysis is needed to establish the degree to which students have achieved the objectives, and the techniques at various stages that were effective in stimulating student learning. Evaluative input will include not only conventional examinations in subject content of the course, but also impressions and comments about the entire unit of study from members of the instructional team and from the students. Then all elements must be reconsidered, to firm up the presentations that were most successful, and to redesign or substitute for elements that missed the mark.

The basic purpose of the systematic approach to instruction is to enable all parts of the learning system to work together toward clearly stated and agreed upon goals, so that both instructor failure to teach and student failure to learn may be practically eliminated. Precise planning is needed if these results are to be approximated, and constant feedback and replanning are essential. But the outcomes in effectiveness and relevance of instruction are well worth the effort expended. Chapter Six is concerned entirely with the techniques of evaluation in the instructional system.

## SUMMARY

The systematic concept of instruction is a recognition that organized opportunity for learning comprises several functions, the talents of several kinds of human specialists, and the contributions of recently invented communications media as well as those of the printed word. In the schema presented in Chapter Three, six aspects of college teaching were discussed as parts of the system:

(1) the purposes of instruction, to be stated as intended changes in the behavior of students (terminal behavior)
(2) the entering behaviors of the students in relation to the purposes of the course
(3) the instructional personnel available to prepare and present the activities of the course

(4) the nonhuman resources provided or obtainable
(5) the logistic capability of the institution, to bring together in the right place at the right time and in appropriate combinations each of the preceding elements
(6) program evaluation, feedback, and improvement.

Throughout Chapter Three, systematic analysis was stressed as a means to enhance the interpersonal contribution of the professor by using alternative techniques to accomplish informational, skill, or appreciation objectives. The total instructional system is effective only to the extent that it provides better achievement of such objectives by greater numbers of students.

## RELATED READING

Banathy, Bela. *Instructional Systems.* Palo Alto, Calif: Fearon Publishers, 1968.

Bloom, Benjamin S., et al. *Taxonomy of Educational Objectives.* New York: David McKay Company, Inc., 1956.

Briggs, Leslie J. *Sequencing of Instruction in Relation to Hierarchies of Competence.* Pittsburgh: American Institutes for Research, 1968.

Bushnell, Don, and Dwight Allen (eds.). *The Computer in American Education.* New York: John Wiley and Sons, Inc., 1967.

Dressel, Paul L., and Francis DeLisle. *Undergraduate Curriculum Trends.* Washington: American Council on Education, 1969.

Dubin, Robert, and Thomas Taveggia. *The Teaching-Learning Paradox: A Comparative Analysis of College Teaching.* Eugene, Oregon: Center for the Advanced Study of Educational Administration, University of Oregon, 1968.

Evans, Richard L., and Peter K. Leppman. *Resistance to Innovation in Higher Education.* San Francisco: Jossey-Bass, Inc., 1967.

Gagne, Robert M. *The Conditions of Learning.* New York: Holt, Rinehart and Winston, 1965.

Hilgard, Ernest R. (ed.). *Theories of Learning and Instruction.* Sixty-sixth Yearbook of the National Society for the Study of Education, Part II. Chicago: University of Chicago Press, 1967.

Jackson, Philip W. *The Teacher and the Machine.* Pittsburgh: University of Pittsburgh Press, 1968.

Johnson, B. Lamar. *Islands of Innovation Expanding: Changes in the Community Colleges.* Beverly Hills, Calif.: Glencoe Press, 1969.

Krathwohl, David R., Benjamin S. Bloom, and Bertram B. Masia. *Taxonomy of Educational Objectives, The Classification of Educational Goals. Handbook II: Affective Domain,* New York: David McKay Company, Inc., 1964.

Loughary, John W. *Man-Machine Systems in Education.* New York: Harper and Row, 1966.

Mackenzie, Norman, Michael Eraut, and Hywel C. Jones. *Teaching and Learning: An Introduction to New Methods and Resources in Higher Education,* Paris: United Nations Educational, Scientific, and Cultural Organizations, and the International Association of Universities, 1970.

McLuhan, Marshall. *Understanding Media.* New York: McGraw-Hill Book Company, 1964.

Mager, Robert F. *Developing Attitude toward Learning.* Palo Alto, Calif.: Fearon Publishers, 1968.

Mager, Robert F. *Preparing Educational Objectives.* Palo Alto, Calif.: Fearon Publishers, 1964.

Skinner, B. F., *The Technology of Teaching.* New York: Appleton-Century-Crofts, 1968.

Smith, Robert G., Jr. *The Design of Instructional Systems.* Washington: Human Resource Office, George Washington University, 1966.

Thornton, James W., Jr., and James W. Brown. *New Media and College Teaching.* Washington: American Association for Higher Education, 1968.

# chapter four / TEACHING AND LEARNING MODES / LARGE GROUP INSTRUCTION • MEDI-UM-GROUP INSTRUCTION • SMALL-GROUP INSTRUCTION • INDEPENDENT STUDY • THE POSTLETHWAIT AUDIO-TUTORI-AL PLAN • SUMMARY • RELATED READING

The preceding chapter set the stage for the following discussion of systematic uses of alternative teaching-learning modes. The faculty member systematically planning a course for the first time will recognize that he must make several important decisions. A number of these decisions will have been made for him by virtue of administrative arrangements within the institution itself. Yet the instructor will still be responsible for selecting the specific activities in which he will engage and those in which his students will engage to meet the requirements of his course. He will be helped in all such decisions by carefully considering the applicability of various teaching and learning activities to his particular discipline, as well as the most suitable physical environments and teaching formats in which to conduct them.

This chapter examines unique features of four different modes of college teaching: (1) large-group, which often involves team teaching, (2) medium-group, (3) small-group, and (4) independent study. The first three of these modes usually involve in-person contributions of professors at the scene of instruction; with the fourth, individual students pursue learning largely on their own.

A recent report of the Instructional Technology Committee of the National Academy of Engineering[1] places these four alternative approaches to higher education in perspective:

[1] John R. Whinnery (Chairman), *Educational Technology in Higher Education* (Washington: Commission on Education of the National Academy of Engineering, 1969), p. 14.

. . . The attempt to develop a standard method of instruction for all courses is giving way to the realization that it is best to provide students a variety of learning situations during their university careers. These learning situations should include live lecturers in large groups, lecture groups in medium sized groups and televised instruction in small rooms but with large numbers of students per course. They should also include laboratory experiences, small study discussion groups using student leaders, a few small seminars with outstanding professors and, finally, independent study. Some ITV courses may use only TV presentations. In other cases, the TV presentations will be complemented with tutorial discussions or laboratory activities. Exposing students to this variety of learning situations, including ITV, gives them the best possibility of developing a variety of learning skills to transfer to the outside world where knowledge is acquired under all of the above conditions.

## LARGE-GROUP INSTRUCTION

Large-group instruction, a common teaching mode in American higher education, has often been criticized for being too impersonal and dehumanized, but imaginative examples show that these are not necessary outcomes. Large-group instruction can be made a very effective means for providing at least part of the education of today's college and university students.

The number of students now in higher education is dramatically greater than the figure of only a few years ago. This increase in numbers has increased the pressure upon institutional finances. There is a continuing need for more money to hire more faculty, to pay them better salaries, to construct more buildings, and to provide the variety of materials and technological devices that modern instruction requires.

Partly as a consequence of such pressures, both research foundations and many colleges and universities have given renewed attention to experiments making large-group teaching methods effective and attractive to students and faculty.

### LARGE-GROUP LECTURING, WITHOUT MEDIA

The formal lecture before groups of several hundred students, given without media support, continues to be a widely used instructional format in higher education. It is the original model of large-group teaching. While many recent technological developments (multi-screen projection arrangements, computer-managed instruction and response units, and the like) have served to extend the range and effectiveness of the lecturer, it is nevertheless true that most large-group teaching is still done without such reinforcement.

Many professors (but probably much smaller percentages of students) regard solo, nonmediated lecturing as the best method for clearly organized presentations and explanations before large groups. In his summary of research comparing lecturing and the discussion methods, McKeachie asked:

> What can be said about lectures versus discussion? Since discussion offers the opportunity for a good deal of student activity and feedback, it could be (according to theory) and is (according to research results) more effective than typical lectures in developing concepts and problem-solving skills. However, because the rate of transmission of information is slow in discussion classes, we would expect lecture classes to be superior in attaining the objective of teaching knowledge. Research results tend to support this generalization and probably are not more convincing largely because the knowledge tested on course examinations usually can be learned by reading the textbook.[2]

Barzun argues strongly for use of the formal, nonmediated lecture in college teaching. He says:

> The lecture room is the place where drama may properly become theater. This usually means a fluent speaker, no notes, and no shyness about "effects." In some teachers a large class filling a sloped-up amphitheater brings out a wonderful power of emphasis, timing, and organization. . . . The "effects" are not laid on, they are the meaningful stress which constitutes, most literally, the truth of the matter. This meaning as against fact is the one thing to be indelibly stamped on the mind, and it is this that the printed book cannot give. That is why their hearers never forgot Huxley lecturing, nor Michelet, nor William James. Plenty of facts can be conveyed, too—the more highly organized the better; but in the hands of a great lecturer it is feeling and principles that illuminate the soul as does a perfect play or concert.[3]

[2]W. J. McKeachie, "Research In Teaching: The Gap Between Theory and Practice," in *Improving College Teaching*, ed. Calvin B.T. Lee (Washington: American Council on Education, 1967), p. 216.

[3]Jacques Barzun, *Teacher in America* (Boston: Atlantic Monthly Press, 1944), p. 38. Copyright 1944, 1945 by Jacques Barzun; by permission of Little, Brown and Company.

The value of the formal, nonmediated lecture seems to depend more upon the special abilities and qualifications of the individual who develops and delivers it than upon advantages or disadvantages inherent in the method itself. The well-prepared lecturer who is familiar with the backgrounds and special needs of his students, for example, may provide through his presentations unique contributions to learning. He may select significant elements and ignore or play down others. Were his students to attempt to read these same points in ordinary (not specially edited) printed materials, they might require more time and find difficulty in separating the essential from the nonessential. By adding to such points the emphasis of his own personality (lending, in the process, additional credibility) he may increase learning or effect changes in attitudes or values.

Several specific suggestions may help the lecturer to improve techniques of planning and delivering formal, nonmediated lectures:

By all means, remember that teaching is not synonymous with telling or describing. The purposes of the lecture are to summarize, to clarify, to stimulate, to humanize the materials of the course. It should synthesize, evaluate, criticize, and compare ideas and facts with which students have come in contact through out-of-class assignments.

Introduce the lecture with a brief review of the work preceding. Indicate how the day's lecture fits into the course pattern.

Narrow the lecture content to essential points that can be treated well rather than make a superficial survey of more than can be grasped in the period.

As examples and illustrations of lecture points, use items that touch the backgrounds and experiences of the students. Plan use of examples in advance.

Do not read the lecture. Make it as personal as possible, not obviously filtered through notes. Glance frequently at students in various parts of the room to assess reactions and probable comprehension. Repeat or rephrase obviously confused points. Pace delivery to allow the majority of students to follow.

Give attention to voice control. Avoid monotonal expression; speak loudly enough to be heard in all parts of the room.

Communicate enthusiasm for the subject.

Even when discussion and oral reaction are not feasible or intended, use rhetorical questions to stimulate thinking.

Summarize at the end of the lecture to review its main points; suggest the nature of the following period's work with suitable transitional comments.

**Figure 4-1.**

## MEDIATED LARGE-GROUP LECTURING

Mediated large-group lecturing involves the use of a variety of communication materials and devices to demonstrate, elaborate upon, or sometimes even substitute entirely for the professor's own comments and explanations. Appropriate visual, audio, or electronic feedback materials and devices are used by the lecturer in order to provide a smooth-flowing presentation that achieves clear communication of ideas and proceeds efficiently toward well-defined ends.

Figures 4-1, 4-2, 4-3, and 4-4 illustrate a physical plant designed for large group teaching at Pennsylvania State University.[4] There, an instructional building known as The Forum has been in use for several years. The design of the building, which includes four large lecture halls each seating 395 students, gave special attention to characteristics believed to relate to effective teaching and learning for large groups of students.

The building is circular in shape and has a central core which contains on the upper level equipment for projecting 2-by-2-inch, 3¼-by-4-inch slides, 16mm films, and television. The building is arranged to provide for rear projection on a translucent screen in each of the four auditoriums. Each screen is 14 feet wide

[4]Details of The Forum prepared by Dr. Leslie P. Greenhill, Assistant Vice President for Resident Instruction, Pennsylvania State University.

**Figure 4-2.**

and 7 feet high and will accommodate two images side by side or a central image.

The projection equipment is located perpendicular to the axis of the screen. Slides are loaded in reverse to appear correctly oriented on the screen. The image from each 16mm projector is reversed by means of a small front surface mirror located close to the projector lens. All projection equipment in this central core is operated by the instructor from a simple control panel on his lectern; it can also be controlled by a technician from a remote location.

Facilities also exist for audio recording and playback, and a small television camera is available to each auditorium for the magnification of small objects or for televising demonstrations. The image from the television camera appears via a television projector on the large translucent screen. In each auditorium a front projection screen is also available for the use of an overhead projector.

Special attention was given to sight lines from the audience and to lighting in the auditorium. The chalkboard is illuminated with regular fluorescent lights, and with ultraviolet lights for use of fluorescent chalk. The general room lighting units are on a series of circuits which can be preset for various viewing

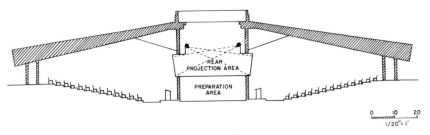

REAR
PROJECTION AREA

PREPARATION
AREA

0    10    20

1/20"= 1'

Figure 4-3.

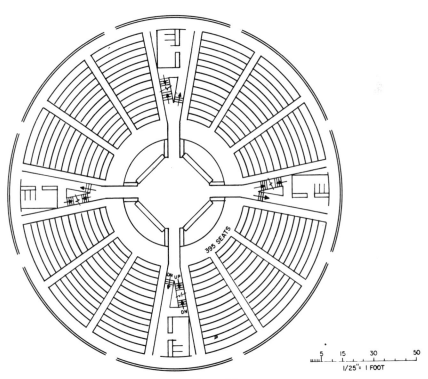

395 SEATS

ON UP

DN

5    15    30    50

1/25"= 1 FOOT

Figure 4-4.

87

conditions and a master switch is then used to activate the preset combination.

The architect gave considerable attention to the acoustical characteristics of the rooms to ensure good audibility of the spoken word and projected sound, The ceiling and sidewalls have hard, sound-reflecting surfaces, the rear walls and seats are sound-absorptive. In actual use the acoustics of the rooms is excellent.

In the central core below the projection area is a preparation and storage room for instructional equipment and materials. Between the segments of the building occupied by the auditoriums are rest rooms at one level and equipment for the air-conditioning system at the upper level.

One of the rooms is equipped with a "wet" demonstration table for science instruction; two of the other rooms have additional motorized chalkboards for use in some courses.

Mediated large-group teaching usually involves organizing an instructional team. Under this plan, two or more instructors (and possibly other supporting specialist personnel) are assigned to work together in teaching the same group of students. Their work may be divided in any one of several ways, but the most common pattern is to have different instructors take specialized responsibilities for special portions or activities of the course. Staff economies are sought by combining separate, small classes into one large class or by teaching students alternately first in one large class and subsequently in smaller groups, as dictated by their activities.

In the opinion of its supporters, large-group team teaching offers a number of advantages:

Individual instructors are given opportunities to specialize in those aspects of a course for which they are best qualified.

Instructors are allowed more time to prepare, under this plan, than when they have the entire responsibility for a class.

Instructors are stimulated to do better teaching by close association with other members of the team; they learn much about teaching by observing, discussing, and working out course problems with their colleagues.

Students are stimulated by the variety of points of view and instructor personalities to which they are exposed.

Time becomes available to prepare or to utilize teaching techniques which require considerable advance preparation (resource persons, films, transparencies and slides, charts, recordings).

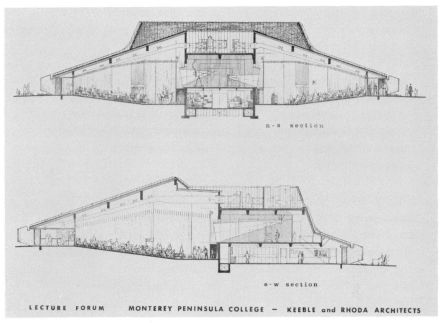

n-s section

e-w section

LECTURE FORUM   MONTEREY PENINSULA COLLEGE — KEEBLE and RHODA ARCHITECTS

**Figure 4-5.**
The Lecture-Forum Building at Monterey Peninsula College (California) provides numerous opportunities for systematically mediating teaching-learning experiences.

Economies are effected in many teaching activities (e.g., preparation, administration, and scoring of tests).

The Lecture-Forum Building at the Monterey Peninsula College, Monterey, California, represents a facility which has been specially designed and equipped to accommodate mediated large-group team teaching.[5] Emphasis there is upon "twentieth century" lectures which substitute for the common dependence on talk alone the liberal use of visual and audio materials that are woven smoothly into all presentations. In the Monterey Peninsula College Plan, considerable emphasis is placed upon course design. The model for these activities is a local adaptation of the one developed by Leslie J. Briggs[6] which involves:

[5] Described in Leon J. Fletcher, "Preparing for 20th Century Lectures," *Audiovisual Instruction* vol. 13 (November 1968):974-977.

[6] Leslie J. Briggs, *A Procedure for the Design of Multi-Media Instruction* (Pittsburgh: American Institutes for Research, 1968).

Specifying behavioral objectives (with performance specifications)

Sequencing objectives so basic knowledge is acquired prior to more complex learning

Identifying each objective element which can be learned effectively (and economically) in large-group, multi-media reinforced teaching sessions

Selecting and/or designing and producing a suitable variety of educational media to facilitate such learning

Planning to use discussions, reading assignments, independent study, or other means to teach concepts appearing to be least suited to learning in the large-group format

The Monterey Peninsula College Forum Building contains three large-group rooms seating 259, 159, and 107 students. The two larger rooms have theater-type chairs with retractable tablet arms; continuous tables in the smaller room provide space for student workbooks, guides, artifacts, and other materials to be consulted or examined during lecture-demonstrations. Three projection screens are provided in each room. Two polarized glass screens are used for rear-projection of films, slides, or filmstrips; a front-projection screen is used for overhead transparencies. The advantage of rear-screen projection is that lights need not be dimmed low, as is required for front projection. Students may thus take notes without difficulty and instructors are able to maintain visual contact as the presentation proceeds.

The Forum Building also features remote controls at the rostrum permitting instructors to start and stop projectors or tape recorders and to control sound sources. Wireless microphones allow instructors to move about freely during presentations. Sloped floors provide good sight-lines from all parts of the rooms; a flat floor at the front of each room permits the rolling in of carts or tables containing demonstration equipment. Continuous feedback from students is being studied experimentally through use of an electronic student-response system. Technician services are available, as necessary, to handle setup and operation of audiovisual equipment.

Space is also provided in the Forum Building for preparation of media to be used in connection with large-group presentations. A graphic artist assists instructors in preparing charts, signs, cartoons, graphs, drawings, and the like; a photographer is available to make slides of materials from books, magazines, or other sources. Video and audio recording and duplicating are offered as additional services. Typing and duplicating services are available to instructors wishing to prepare student handouts.

### OTHER LARGE-GROUP TEACHING FORMATS

Three additional large-group teaching formats should be mentioned:

The in-person *forum-lecture* is widely used with large groups, especially in auditorium situations in which facilities exist to provide amplification of questions and comments from the floor. With this teaching format, the lecturer presents his message without interruption, often including visual or demonstration materials. This is followed by a period for questions from the floor. Sometimes listeners are asked to write questions on cards during the lecture. A chairman or observer usually selects and reads questions, as time permits, and summarizes at the end.

Another variation of this procedure is provided by the *symposium* or *town meeting*. With either, the usual custom is to present statements of several persons who hold different points of view about the subject under consideration. Each presents his ideas in a short speech. The moderator then opens the meeting to questions from the floor.

A variation of the in-person forum-lecture format, discussed above, is the *amplified telephone interview* or *telelecture*. With either of these arrangements, colleges avail themselves of the instructional contributions of guests who cannot come to their campuses, but who are willing to devote time to a telephone dialogue with a remote class. Visitors from abroad or important governmental or scientific personalities who cannot be present in person, may be prevailed upon to use a telephone in their own homes or offices and be interviewed for instructional purposes.

Burkhart studied telelecture techniques. He concluded that:

Classroom interviews are not self-operating. The teacher must be thoroughly familiar with the topic or area of discussion, must know something about the background of the interviewee, and be prepared to direct the discussion along profitable lines, preventing it from becoming just another "bull session." To do this requires knowledge and skill on the part of the instructor. Associated with the larger and more difficult role played by the instructor is his personal involvement in the interview. Frequently the intellectual excitement is so great that the teacher is literally worn out at the end of the class session.[7]

[7]James A. Burkhart, "An Experiment to Determine the Values of Using Amplified Classroom Telephone Interviews with Significant Individuals to Enrich Certain College Courses" (Ph.D. diss., University of Missouri, 1960).

## MEDIUM-GROUP INSTRUCTION

Groups of from thirty-five to sixty students continue to be a popular class size despite the increased attention to large-group instruction just discussed. Informal lecturing, group discussion, role playing, demonstrations, laboratory instruction, and field trips and community study, as discussed here, represent various means of achieving instructional purposes with such medium-sized groups.

### INFORMAL LECTURING

Mayhew makes the point that "the trouble with many lecturers is that they insist on providing all the answers, leaving nothing for the students to do."[8] He suggests, instead, that the adroit lecturer ought to provide some evidence, raise some questions, point out some possible conclusions, and then leave the students to follow up and reach their own conclusions. The informal lecture, carried on in medium-sized groups, meets many of these requirements. It provides opportunities for students to participate by commenting about points in the lecture or answering questions thrown out by other students in the class.

Suggestions following are intended to aid in improving informal lecturing as a method of teaching:

Pre-plan provocative questions that will form the basis for good discussion. Experiment with their use before or after related points have been developed in the lecture.

State the question; then seek a volunteer for an answer, or call on a specific student. This practice tends to insure a greater degree of attention since anyone may be called on.

Study student reactions as the lecture or discussion proceeds. Shift activity from lecturing to discussing, as appropriate, to emphasize points and to retain attention. Sample comprehension, from time to time, by asking one or more students to recapitulate a main point covered.

Ask for a show of hands occasionally, to sample student opinions about points under consideration.

Invite volunteers, or call on students to provide examples that support, qualify, or contradict points made in the lecture.

Spread participation in discussion to as many class members as possible.

Give students enough time to answer questions before moving on to someone else. Hear out a student's comments (unless they ramble); then ask others to react—to agree, disagree, qualify, or supplement.

[8]Lewis B. Mayhew, *General Education: An Account and Appraisal* (New York: Harper & Row, Publishers, Inc., 1960), p. 96.

Acknowledge student answers or comments by some appropriate remark. If they are obviously off the track, return the discussion to the main point and proceed.

Call on students in random, not alphabetical, order. At the same time, consider keeping some check on the frequency with which different students volunteer or are called on. A code system of circles, checks, plus or minus signs, or similar marks can be used for this purpose. Evaluations of adequacy of performance can also be recorded in this manner.

Accustom students to listening carefully so questions need not be repeated. If a question is repeated, it should be for emphasis or clarity, as in the case of paraphrasing or asking it differently.

From time to time, insert a period of silence and wait for response; or ask rhetorical questions in various parts of the lecture.

## MEDIUM-GROUP DISCUSSION PATTERNS

Several discussion patterns—panel discussion, debate discussion, dialogue, buzz groups, and brainstorming—are rather widely used in medium-group instruction. With *panel discussions,* a small group of persons (typically from three to six) who have some expertness in the subject talk about a problem before the class. No one makes a speech. Rather, there is interplay back and forth among the panel members—with agreement, disagreement, qualification, point elaboration. A panel chairman participates, as needed, to keep discussion to the point, to invite nonparticipants to talk, or to give an occasional summary to suggest how the discussion has progressed. The emphasis in panel discussions is upon trying to solve problems through reflective group thinking. Once the panel has made its presentation, others of the class may be invited to ask questions or to make comments or observations. The chairman usually makes an appropriate summary at the end.

*Debate discussion* is related in form to the panel discussion, but with this method two or more speakers usually take definite points of view, present their opinions and facts, and participate later by responding to questions or comments from others in the class. Debate discussion is a useful device for stimulating student participation in discussions; it helps, also, to identify arguments which support differing points of view. It does emphasize competition and winning an argument rather than a scholarly search for agreement.

*Dialogue* uses an expert and an expert interviewer to explore a subject prior to its later discussion by the entire class. The expert may be a well-informed student, a member of the faculty, or a person drawn from the community, such

**Figure 4-6.**
The inexpensive cassette tape recorder proves to be especially useful in facilitating the summarization of small group discussions and committee deliberations for later presentation to large groups of students.

as from some government agency; the interviewer may be the instructor or a class member. The interviewer is presumably familiar with the special interests of the class with regard to the subject under discussion. He has previously alerted the expert to these interests, and his questions draw comments related particularly to these points. Time is left in the period to invite questions and comments from the class. A summation is made by either the interviewer or an observer.

*Buzz groups* are commonly used with medium groups (and sometimes with large groups) to obtain maximum student participation in discussions. Typically, a presentation is first made to the class. The chairman then asks the group to divide into subgroups of six or seven (three in one row and three or four in the row directly behind). Subgroups are then given a minute or so in which to select a discussion leader and a reporter. The subgroup discussion leader assumes responsibility for seeing that each member of the group expresses himself about the presentation just made. After a few minutes, subgroups are usually re-formed into the original large group. The reporter of each such subgroup is then asked to give a short summary of reactions to the presentation and to present to the expert or panel questions raised in his group. These may be answered as they are presented or after all subgroups have reported.

*Brainstorming* is another discussion form which enables groups to do collective creative thinking. Emphasis here is placed upon eliciting a number of ideas for later more careful consideration. With brainstorming, the mind is stimulated to think without inhibition. Ideas are never rejected *during* the process, however inept or unpromising they appear to be; they are sorted out and evaluated later. Adapting and elaborating upon ideas suggested by others is encouraged. The suggestion of one member leads to elaboration by another, until the level of creativity is limited only by the enthusiasm of the group.

### ROLE PLAYING

Role playing[9] as sometimes used in college classes is a means of providing spontaneous, unrehearsed, lifelike representations of experience for various teaching and learning objectives. The technique has been found useful for

Helping students see ways of applying principles studied in the abstract
Enabling students to understand motivations of other persons by acting out
    those persons' roles
Heightening student awareness of psychological and social problems
Adding realism and variety to course activities

Simple role playing may be conducted with groups of varying size, from the small seminar to the large lecture class. The process starts with the selection of an appropriate problem situation. The best problems are those that deal with human relations—the actions, beliefs, and values of people. Problems may be suggested by readings (including case studies), films, news stories, recordings, or TV presentations.

In setting up role-playing situations, the following steps and procedures are suggested:

*Isolate the problem, and set the stage.* Careful preliminary planning and study of the problem to be role-played will help to avoid last-minute difficulties. Decide what roles are needed; give thought to persons in the class who might

---

[9] Psychodrama, a more technical and complicated form of role playing sometimes used for therapy with certain kinds of personality disorders, is not to be discussed here.

play them most effectively. Decide, too, whether certain props will be needed. Explain to the class in advance about the situation to be role played, describing generally what is to be done and its importance as a learning activity.

*Call for volunteers, or make assignments for the roles to be played.* This may be done before class or somewhat spontaneously as the role-playing session starts. It is more likely that a successful dramatization will occur if each student understands the role he is to play and if he is able to project his personality before groups without embarrassment or undue inhibition. The playing group sometimes meets alone for a few minutes and organizes its plans while the instructor explains details to the rest of the class.

*Role play the incident.* Ask the role-playing group to begin the dramatization. The rest of the class watches as a single group, although selected individuals may be asked to give particular attention to specific aspects of the presentation. While spontaneity is encouraged, players should be expected to stay within their roles. The play should be allowed to proceed without interruption for probably no more than three to six minutes, when, if it has not already come to a logical stopping point, the instructor will close it off.

*Discuss the presentation.* A discussion of the role-playing presentation may begin by asking participants themselves to evaluate the execution of their roles. Then the discussion may be taken over by the class—as a single group or as separate buzz groups. The student analysis may properly include efforts to identify strengths or weaknesses of roles (not in the manner in which they were played but in what was said or otherwise communicated), applications of principles involved, and contributions of role playing to the solution of the original problem.

## DEMONSTRATIONS

Demonstrations are widely used in college teaching, especially in medium-group teaching. They help to focus attention on steps and procedures involved in executing various manual operations (as in staining tissues or bending glass tubing), in various performing arts (painting, singing, or dancing), in science or engineering (step-by-step demonstrations of physical or chemical phenomena), and for numerous other purposes.

Suggestions for more effective instructor demonstrations follow:

*Determine specifically the objectives and content of the demonstration.* The instructor needs a clear grasp of the present level of understanding or skills already possessed by students. Decide at this point what key terms, ideas, principles, or questions will be introduced.

*Explain the purposes of the demonstration* and the expected outcomes.

*Make an advance trial run, if possible.* This procedure will help to ensure that all necessary materials, equipment, and facilities are available and operating, that timing is appropriate, and that unanticipated problems will be uncovered.

*Plan ways of retaining attention.* Good showmanship is critical in demonstrations. The instructor may wonder out loud, for example, asking questions such as, "If I move this dial, what will happen?" He may also keep demonstration materials out of sight until they are needed. He will be certain, too, that everyone is able to see and hear. Closed-circuit TV cameras and receivers in the demonstration room are especially helpful here.

*Pace the demonstration* to enable most persons to follow it. Watch facial expressions for signs of confusion; check understandings from time to time to determine whether points should be repeated.

*Invite participation,* as appropriate, through questions or invitations to students to attempt operations demonstrated.

*Summarize, discuss, and evaluate the discussion.* At the end of the demonstration, review key points, invite questions, attempt to clear up misconceptions, and evaluate what has been learned.

*Use videotaping techniques* to compress certain lengthy demonstrations into a class period by eliminating unproductive time (as when water is coming to a boil, or an egg is hatching, and so on).

### LABORATORY INSTRUCTION

One important function of laboratory instruction is to give students real experiences and to allow them to discover things for themselves, whether or not those same things have already been discovered by others. It also helps students to develop skill in stating and delimiting problems, controlling conditions, making measurements, treating and interpreting data, and drawing conclusions.

Genuine laboratory instruction is difficult (and often expensive) to administer. For these reasons, pressure is sometimes exerted to substitute in its place highly structured "cookbook" exercises that are pseudo forms of experimentation. Genuine discovery or problem-solving laboratory experiences are generally preferred to the structured types. They can help to minimize the idea that the

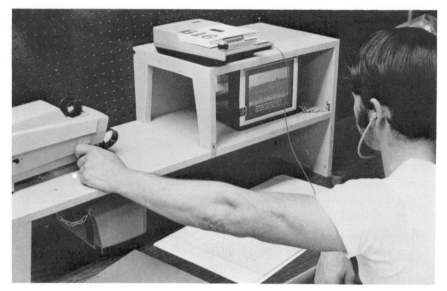

**Figure 4-7.**
Combinations of programmed manuals, natural color filmstrips, and cassette tape recordings containing instructor comments sometimes replace the ordinary laboratory instruction of college science classes.

scientific method is a magical route to scientific discovery. It becomes, instead, a method whose effectiveness is determined to a large extent by the care with which disciplined, but often quite ordinary, persons find answers to ordinary as well as extraordinary problems.

Broadly defined, laboratory experience is possible as a learning activity for practically any college course, not just for the sciences or applied arts. Opportunities are numerous for students to have profitable firsthand contacts with unanalyzed data and with a variety of primary sources. A course in elementary economics might include such varied experiences as field trips to banks or stock exchanges, including interviews with employees, inspections of the accounts of small businesses, or work experience in government regulatory agencies. A course in human geography might include laboratory experiences in map and chart production, field trip observations, interviews, photographing, analysis of photographs, and tape recording or analyzing interviews. In all such instances, the laboratory becomes the place in which theoretical aspects of a subject are tempered by practical experience. In the light of the current trend toward teaching in larger groups by means of television and other new media, the personal and independent laboratory experience is an important means of emphasizing activity rather than receptivity as a learning mode.

## FIELD TRIPS AND COMMUNITY STUDY

Field trips, community study, and community resources also help to enrich instruction by introducing practical aspects of the subject as applications of classroom theory. Field trips and community study permit students to analyze problems in fairly unstructured ways; in the process they are expected to exercise judgment and evolve conclusions about meanings or results of their study.

There are several serious problems connected with field trips, even in higher education, with which the instructor must be concerned. There is first the matter of institutional policy pertaining to requiring the attendance of students at off-campus field trip locations. In most institutions, procedures and requirements with respect to field trips have been detailed for the general guidance of the faculty. It is the instructor's responsibility to ascertain and to follow the guidelines to avoid the personal liability of claims for damage resulting from accidents. Secondly, there is the matter of timing; unless the trip can be completed within the time usually allotted to the class, the instructor must often obtain official excuses from classes with conflicting schedules.

Successful field trips require considerable planning and effort. Assuming the proposed trip is essential and that a suitable destination is selected, the instructor has several responsibilities. He must:

*Make preliminary contacts with officials or others at the destination site.* It is usually recommended that the instructor himself visit the location before going there with his class.

*Make final arrangements with the college or university officials* as to liability coverage, absence of students, and other matters. The filling out of certain forms is usually required.

*Prepare a guide sheet* for members of the class, to be handed out well in advance of the trip. Such guide sheets often contain full details of trip location, departure and arrival times, return times, route descriptions, major purposes of the trip (including significant features or operations to study most carefully), costs (if any), recommended clothing, names of individuals at the destination site, and safety rules, as needed. A copy of this guide sheet should also be given to the destination officials to alert them to emphases intended. It is also recommended that there be some preliminary discussion of the guide sheet with the class, perhaps at its meeting the day before the trip. Certain class members may at that time be given special assignments (arrangements, collecting money, giving attention to one particular aspect of the visit to report on at the next class session, or others). It is also recommended that decisions be made, before departure, about important questions to be asked at the destination site and perhaps the names of individuals to ask them.

*Prepare a follow-up discussion and evaluation* of the field trip for the next session of the class. The follow-up should relate to the major questions and to study points mentioned in the trip guide.

Many institutions have established community projects to provide liaison between the practical and the theoretical in the fields of education and sociology. Such projects include surveys of living and health conditions in homes of members of minority groups, opinion surveys, or consumer-interest inventories. In some cases, class members are organized for house-to-house interviews. In others, individuals are asked to study some community agency and to report findings. One- or two-page summaries of reports are duplicated for other class members to provide current data about agencies studied.

Various other community resources for college teaching merit serious consideration. Some valuable resources are individuals who live or work within reach of the college. These are the professional specialists (editors, writers, doctors, engineers, law enforcement officials, social workers, and others). They comprise a reservoir of experts who are willing to serve as voluntary consultants for classroom lectures or demonstrations. Many institutions provide funds for honorariums for such participation.

Again, as with field trips, advance arrangements must be made to ensure adequate use of the talents of such persons. The instructor (or one or more students) should:

Interview the expert, after the first preliminary contact, and explain fully the intended purposes of his visit to the class. Leaving a list of important questions which the class wishes to have answered is a help in focusing his contributions.

Explain (preferably in writing) the exact details of time, room location, length of participation, and type of participation expected. Such presentations often take the form of interviews.

Arrange to follow up the classroom appearance with a letter of appreciation or telephone call.

## SMALL-GROUP INSTRUCTION

Small-group instruction, conducted in groups ranging from approximately five to fifteen persons, is expected to provide maximum opportunity for instructor-student and student-student interaction. Both appear to be highly regarded by students. Two teaching and learning activities found to be especially compatible to achievement of objectives in small-group instruction are the *discussion* and the *seminar*.

### SMALL-GROUP DISCUSSION

Continued emphasis in college teaching upon developing powers of critical thinking and problem solving, accounts, in part, for current attention to the method of group discussion. Small-group discussion is widely regarded as basic to the democratic process. It is neither persuasion nor debate; rather, it is a group effort to think and reflect collectively. The term itself identifies a technique that may involve an entire medium-group class, or perhaps only part of a class, depending upon circumstances. Although group members may approach a discussion problem from varying points of view, effort is made to examine it in ways calculated to demonstrate effective thinking. Eventual judgments or decisions relating to such problems are no single person's view or idea; they are a reasonable composite of all of them. Insight rather than conquest of opponents is the goal.

Probably the single most important requirement of an effective small-group discussion is to select a good discussion problem. Such a problem appears to be most satisfactory when it is: (1) related to something about which the students already have background and experience, but on which they need additional emphasis; (2) of interest to the discussants—regarded as significant and worth consideration; (3) novel enough to hold interest—not stale because of overuse; (4) somewhat controversial and incapable of being answered by a yes or no; and (5) sufficiently limited in scope to be discussed in the time available.

In leading group discussions, the instructor will need to:

Build upon common experiences and understandings. This may involve a previous reading assignment, or a film used to present the discussion stimulus during the first part of the class period.

Clarify and restrict the discussion topic or problem so that it is understood and capable of being discussed in the time allotted. Identify assumptions and subproblems. Settle upon an order of discussion.

Clarify procedures—how the discussion will be conducted, when it will conclude, what it will seek to accomplish.

Allow the discussion to veer from course when such a step promises to be fruitful. But be ready to come back to the original point when the detour has served its purpose.

Build a spirit of group cooperation and friendliness rather than allowing sides to be taken on issues. When arguments do arise and cannot be settled, reserve them or treat them as assumptions and continue. But do not hesitate to encourage differing points of view or occasionally to play the "devil's advocate," where this will prove effective.

Ask questions which elicit facts and opinions, rather than those which can be answered by a yes or no.

Avoid playing a too dominant role in the discussion; put the responsibility on the students. Throw back questions to the group; ask group members to respond to statements of other students.

Summarize from time to time to remind the group of its progress, its unfulfilled commitments, and its remaining time budget.

Restate and clarify contributions, when necessary, to align them with the discussion. Ask students for illustrative examples or restatements so that meanings become clearer.

Recognize varying opinions with regard to the problem under discussion; help to formulate these as minority views.

Leave time for a summary. This may be done by the instructor or by one or more students serving as recorder or observers.

## SEMINARS

One definition of "seminar" describes it as:

> ...a form of class organization in higher education in which a group of advanced graduate students engage in research or advanced study under the

general direction of one or more staff members ... for a discussion of problems of mutual interest.[10]

In actual practice, however, seminar classes may assume any one of several variations of this form. In one, the instructor maintains a fairly tight rein on the proceedings, leading the group through controlled discussion of a series of questions pertaining to the topic while serving at the same time as arbiter and expert judge of the proceedings. This particular seminar form seems well adapted to preparing students for the types of external examinations required for professional certification, or similar purposes.

A second commonly used seminar form involves the instructor in offering a brief preliminary lecture on a topic, chiefly to set the stage and to clarify or delimit issues. His presentation is followed by general discussion by the entire group, based upon a common set of readings or a series of individual investigations or reading assignments. The chief purpose of this discussion is to seek one or more defensible and plausible solutions to the problem. Considerable student participation is expected in planning the agenda and in determining the manner in which such seminar activities are carried out. Occasional meetings of subgroups of seminar participants with the professor may occasionally replace regular seminar sessions.

Several general suggestions to the instructor apply, regardless of the seminar form selected:

Invite student participation in selecting, defining, and delimiting the seminar problems or discussion topics and in providing recommended data or reading sources to accompany them.

Develop student responsibility for making proper preparation in advance of all seminar sessions.

Invite student participation in setting (and clarifying) standards with respect to reports they give and discussions in which they participate.

Avoid the temptation to talk too much, to dominate the discussion, or to take too much time with preliminary lectures.

Use the seminar as a means of developing student awareness and appreciation of the processes of small-group discussion and deliberation. In this connection, audio tape recordings of class sessions may be exceptional sources of data for studying the dynamics of seminar groups.

[10] Carter V. Good, *Dictionary of Education* (New York: McGraw-Hill, 1959), p. 495.

## INDEPENDENT STUDY

Independent study places increased responsibility upon the student for his own education. In the past, this was associated chiefly with honors programs; it is now commonly used as a routine part of the experience of average students as well. Developments and devices that have encouraged wider adoption of independent study in colleges and universities include dial access information retrieval systems (DAIRS), carrel installations ("wet" and/or "dry"; with or without electronic call-up or audiovisual reproduction capabilities), tape and disk listening units, reading and "hard copy" printout facilities for various microforms, computerized and printed programmed instruction, assigned film viewing and individual cartridge-loaded film projectors, games, and simulation devices. New applications appear annually.

Fundamental to all these media and techniques, of course, are the traditional reference materials of the college library.

Arguments are numerous in favor of independent study as a teaching-learning format. Its use enables a student to pursue studies which are often of his own choosing, at his own rate, and to the depth he desires, without specific reference to others enrolled in the course. It is his responsibility to frame the focus of his studies and to budget his time and resources to meet imposed deadlines. In addition, it cultivates the skills and attitudes essential to lifelong learning to which colleges have always given lip service.

So far, it is an illusion to think that widespread use of independent study will necessarily permit an institution to handle more students with the same faculty. Properly organized and conducted, this form of instruction continues to require great instructor commitment of time and effort—sometimes more than the traditional teaching forms.

Several independent study plans are now in common use in institutions of higher learning throughout the country. For example, the student may:[11]

Follow course syllabus assignments for directed reading with little or no instructor contact, except, perhaps, for an initial setting of tasks or a final test of accomplishment.

Have the continuing help of the instructor, or tutor, but operate independently

[11] Adapted from Bruce Dearing, "The Student on His Own: Independent Study," in *Higher Education: Some Newer Developments,* ed. Samuel Baskin (New York: McGraw-Hill, 1965), pp. 53-54.

**Figure 4-8.**
Independent study provided through written and audio assignments is used increasingly in higher education. (Pennsylvania State University)

of a standard syllabus, pursuing his intellectual interests where they take him rather than retracing those of his instructor or of his instructor's instructor.

Be freed from attending a number of his regular class meetings but be expected, nevertheless, to cover, either on his own or in teams or groups with other students, the material that might normally have been covered in the class sessions from which he has been excused.

Work with films, taped lectures, programmed materials, texts, and assigned readings, and be expected to accomplish almost completely on his own the goals usually supported by classroom procedures of lecture and discussion.

Do his independent work off campus, pursuing an individual research project or extramural studies for which he uses field resources.

A "contract" plan is frequently employed to provide scope and logistical organization for processes of independent study. With this plan, the student receives assignments (usually in written form, and often as a result of individual conferences with the instructor) known as contracts or jobs. Details of each assignment are so clearly outlined that a student may work on it independently and at his own speed. Deadline dates set for contract completions are usually spread throughout the term. Students are expected to choose from among alternative contract assignments and to proceed in whatever manner seems most appropriate.

Evaluations of the quality of student work are made, under this plan, as each contract is completed. The overall rating for grading purposes takes into account: (1) the amount of work (number of separate contracts) completed, (2) the quality of completed work, (3) other class contributions, including discussions, and (4) examinations. Contract work is often organized so that minimum *amounts* and *quality* of work must be completed, as scheduled, to earn a particular grade. The points at which such minimums take effect are made clear in the contract-assignment sheets.

The most common types of independent activities, whether in contract or traditional plans, include: (1) assigned reading, (2) assigned listening, (3) assigned viewing—of slides, filmstrips, museum displays, and the like, (4) programmed learning assignments—especially those involving computer-assisted activities, (5) writing assignments, (6) committee assignments, (7) oral reports, (8) creative projects, and (9) work experience and internships.

## ASSIGNED READING

An accepted goal of higher education is that it ought to stimulate students to experience the world's great ideas in ways that help to broaden perspectives and strengthen inner resources. Yet several studies of reading habits conclude that college students often read little beyond materials that are required for their courses. With independent study assignments, however, it becomes possible to expect students to exercise more judgment about book selections, to range more widely in the field of investigation, and to encounter, through this process, sources of ideas that enrich their lives.

While it may be reasonable to expect that a large share of a student's independent reading should be focused by the instructor upon specific requirements of the course, it may also be expected that he will seek consciously to stimulate and encourage other kinds of reading as well. He may carry out this obligation in several ways. He may make a special point, for example, of mentioning or of using apt quotations from books that he himself has read. He may attach an obviously high value to good reading generally. He may leave room in his own reading lists for individual judgment and selection by students and thus encourage library exploration. He may accept and be guided by the point of view that improvement of student reading habits is the responsibility of the entire college teaching staff (including himself).

Students may also be helped to improve their reading habits by coming to understand that there are different kinds of reading for different purposes. Alexander and Burke identify five kinds of reading which should be understood and practiced by college students, as follows:[12]

scanning—as in checking directories or in locating items in a series with the help of mechanical aids

scouting—exploring for valuable references and determining the main features of references

skimming—obtaining the main thoughts or ideas from reading without seeking full details, for some specific purpose

reading thoughtfully or critically—grasping full meaning and solving some problem set up in connection with the reading (following the usual problem-solving procedures referred to earlier)

interpreting—the final stage of reading and the goal of all kinds of reading, applying what is read to one's own problems.

### ASSIGNED LISTENING

Independent listening to prerecorded tapes and disks is on the rise in universities and colleges. This trend has been accelerated by the many recent technological design improvements in related equipment as well as in the format (a move toward easy-to-use cassettes and away from reel-to-reel types) of the tapes themselves. The listening laboratory, which at one time was restricted almost exclusively to foreign language instruction, has now become a more versatile tool. The simplicity, convenience (particularly in cassette form), and minimal cost of reproducing audio tapes make them ideal for use in independent, self-study programs. Current technology provides high-speed tape duplication

[12] Carter Alexander and Arvid J. Burke, *How to Locate Educational Information and Data* (New York: Columbia University, Teachers College, Bureau of Publications, 1958), pp. 159-167.

and random (dial) access to master tape banks with only minimal time delays. With such arrangements, students usually work in carrels; they simply dial appropriate number combinations (obtained from a card catalog or other special directory) to hear the desired program segment. Many hundreds of students may listen to the same tape (and even to different portions of the same tape) at one time without jamming or overloading the system.

Dial access listening facilities also enable students to bring audio learning resources directly into their living quarters (through telephone connections). However, the low-cost, high-quality cassette tape recorder-playback unit offers healthy competition to such developments and may ultimately replace these more complex installations to capture the benefits of individual listening for independent study.

### ASSIGNED VIEWING

Out-of-class viewing of films, filmstrips, slide cartridges, and other visual materials is also important for independent study. Instructors frequently arrange film schedules (complete with time and place data, content synopses, study guide suggestions, and assignments) as required viewing for those enrolled in their classes. Repeated showings, following the predetermined schedule, provide necessary flexibility for such viewing.

Independent viewing of films and other audiovisual materials such as slides or filmstrips is also accomplished by having students check them out (in the same manner as they now check out books) and view them in carrels within the library or learning resources center.

Obviously, such outside viewing assignments must be coordinated with the library or learning resources center, for only then can the instructor be certain that all necessary details are cared for. Students may be helped by use of instructor-prepared viewing or listening guidesheets containing specific titles and call numbers, outlines of content, thought questions or problems, key terms, and similar items.

### PROGRAMMED AND COMPUTERIZED INSTRUCTION[13]

Programmed instruction is a technique of self-instruction that presents instructional experiences in small segments and includes tasks that permit the student to

[13] Materials in this section have been adapted from James W. Brown and James W. Thornton, Jr., *Instructional Uses of Educational Media in Higher Education: A Critique* (USOE, Higher Education Media Study Project, 1967) Chap. 5.

demonstrate his comprehension or skill. If he performs a task correctly, he is immediately presented with another sequence requiring learning-response-judgment; if he then makes an error, he must either restudy the material or "branch" to additional instruction before proceeding. Reinforcement effects of immediate knowledge of success or failure are believed to be powerful stimuli to learning.

Programmed learning may be presented in printed form, in simple or quite complicated teaching machines, by several uses of tapes, by various audiovisual projection or dial-access devices, or by computers. All of these modes are used in higher education. Yet there are no reports indicating that programmed learning is used as the sole model for instruction, without supplement by other methods of presentation or assessment. The task of the professor has nowhere been abdicated entirely to the program. Instead, programs are used to enable the student who needs introductory or remedial work to brush up by himself; more often, they are used as a part of an array of teaching techniques, supplemented variously by lectures, tutors, dial-access tapes, laboratory experiences, alone or in combination. Some of the most successful self-instructional programs appear to be those that require the student at a given point to read in a textbook, view a single-concept film, perform an experiment, or listen to a tape. Except in elementary skill subjects, it is still rare to find a completely self-contained teaching program.

Computers today provide a number of key services related to independent study. In a few colleges and universities, for example, computers are used to provide multiple copies of complete library catalogs which, until now, were available only in card form. Even more significantly, these same computerized data sources can be used to produce selected bibliographic lists related to topics under investigation and thus reduce the time required to track down promising references. Access to data *within* the separate sources, and the capability of providing immediate printouts upon demand, are also possible, but, as yet, not widely used.

With the help of computers, it is possible to present either complete courses or supplementary exercises related to those courses in dialogue form. Such courses can also be made available remotely at a considerable distance from the central computer. Computers are used to provide a record of the successes and difficulties of each student as he works through a programmed course. Such information may be crucial as a basis for improving the course the next time it is used, as well as for counseling the student.

Computerized instructional exercises may be produced as paper printouts (on a machine resembling a typewriter). They may be displayed on a cathode-ray

**Figure 4-9.**
Computers continue to play an increasingly significant role in providing or managing instructional experiences for today's college students.

tube with either verbal or graphic materials, accompanied, possibly, by sound. Students may communicate with the computer by pressing keys, by touching the display screen with a "light pencil," or even by speaking.[14] In the case of the PLATO unit (Programmed Logic for Automatic Teaching Operations), as developed at the University of Illinois, the student communicates with the computer through an adapted electronic typewriter keyboard. In response to typed directions, the computer displays verbal or visual problems. The student types out responses; when he touches a key, a letter or symbol appears on the screen. He completes his response in normal language. When the full response (with the problem) appears on the screen, and when he is ready to have it registered, he touches the "judge" key. Immediately, the computer presents an evaluation of his efforts. This may range from "OK, proceed to the next item" to "Return to frame 20 and begin again." A full record of student responses is

---

[14] Although considerable research has been invested in the development of computers capable of recognizing and analyzing the *content* (message) of human utterances, important breakthroughs in this area are expected to be some time away.

then automatically placed on the computer memory. Subsequently, this record may be summarized for an entire group of participants in one or more sessions or for each separate student who uses the program. Such feedback information is useful to the student (to provide self-study cues to improve performance), as well as to the instructor (to provide reteaching or course improvement cues).

Further suggestions concerning the selection, development, and use of programmed materials in college teaching are provided in the next chapter.

## PAPERS AND WRITTEN REPORTS

Papers and written reports, required almost as frequently as assigned readings and examinations, have certain advantages over other types of independent study assignments. They are individual in nature; students may complete them at their own speed, when and where they choose; they permit students to pursue subjects in which they are genuinely interested; they provide a medium through which students may combine study of facts and ideas with practice in written expression; and they provide the instructor with a student product which can be analyzed, criticized, and rated at his convenience.

Suggestions to instructors about written work assignments for their classes often include the following:

Don't overdo it.

Be reasonable in standards and deadlines; allow sufficient time for students to complete assignments with the care and thoroughness expected.

Make known, in advance, standards by which assignments will be evaluated and rated. Instructors sometimes hand out checksheets to identify evaluative factors.

Make writing assignments learning, not busy-work, assignments; provide suggestions for adequate use of library resources. Students should feel they are writing about something worthwhile.

Select or guide students in selecting important topics. Best topics require students to gather, evaluate, synthesize, and generalize from data and writings they consult, rather than to report or to quote at length from writings of others.

Consider some of the writing and investigative skills of the special field of the course in which the paper is prepared, and explain by use of examples in class. Give suggestions concerning ways to present tabular or graphic data.

Do the students the courtesy of *reading* and *reacting* to their written efforts. Marginal notations and reactions (well beyond the laconic "Inadequate facts" or "Awk.") can convey much to the student and may prove helpful in stimulating improved work in the future.

Several common problems connected with papers and written reports should be mentioned. Papers are sometimes written by willing friends or by commercial ghost writers; they are rewritten from last semester's assignments or cribbed from fraternity files. At times, they are stolen, word for word, from some published work (and woe to the instructor who grades them C—). But perhaps even worse, they are sometimes made of whole cloth—the imaginative work of a creative but misled genius in the third row left.

Instructors intend, of course, that every paper shall be the work of the student who hands it in and that the student will have learned valuable lessons by developing it. There are a few things the teacher may do to further this intention, of which the following are suggestive:

Restrict the list of topics suitable for the assigned paper or report. Some instructors assign all topics; others give a list of suitable topics and ask students to select from it.

Require students to hand in, during the first few weeks after giving the assignment, a tentative outline of the paper and a briefly annotated bibliography which suggests the kinds of background reading already accomplished and still to be accomplished. If the report is to include a survey of the literature, the requirement may be that the survey be completed early and handed in for criticism before the remainder of the paper is written. Time permitting, office interviews with students are recommended. A few well-chosen questions will provide valuable clues as to the authorship of the work.

Decide early, and distribute in mimeographed form, full details of format requirements. Decide, too, the standards for typing versus longhand, and penalties for inadequate proofreading, misspellings, poor organization of ideas, or meager expression,

Include a question about the paper or report in an examination.

Invite all students (in small classes), or in a randomly selected sampling of students (in larger classes), to present brief oral reports and to answer questions about their projects.

## COMMITTEE WORK

Committee work to prepare for a report or a discussion in class is another opportunity for independent study. The development of assignments that are appropriate to committee investigation requires considerable forethought. If committee presentations of findings are to be made, they should be planned carefully to avoid wasting time. Instructors often meet with committees before the presentation. Good committee reports move quickly and in an organized manner toward important, recognized goals. As appropriate, they utilize real things or audiovisual media (charts, displays, slides, blackboard outlines) to improve communication and to heighten interest. They are not allowed to go on interminably; they close on schedule. A summation at the end ties together the ideas developed. Duplicated outlines restating main points are sometimes handed out at that time.

## ORAL REPORTS

Oral reports, occasionally required in college classes, may deal with reviews and critiques, books, the presentation of results of student investigations or research (as in connection with laboratory work), or a combination report-demonstration (such as showing some product developed by a student in the process of solving some problem).

Students should be advised to make adequate notes for their reports, to think of appropriate devices for improving communication and for heightening interest (chalkboard outlines or drawings, charts, overhead transparencies, simple dramatizations), to make their points simply and directly, and, by all means, to respect imposed time limits.

As with other class contributions, oral reports sometimes have a way of getting out of hand. Students become restive (and properly so) when time is wasted by the person who is both unsure of his goals and lacking in communicative skill. The instructor can do much to anticipate such difficulties by monitoring student preparation and by helping the entire class to become aware of presentation standards to be observed.

Tape or videotape recorders may be used to prerecord oral reports in an effort to save class time and, simultaneously, to provide the student with an objective means of mirroring and studying his own performance.

## CREATIVE PROJECTS

Student creative projects in college classes may take a number of different forms; many may be pursued as independent studies. The gradations of originality must be taken into account when judging or commending them. At the lowest level are projects of the "cookbook" variety, made by following specific set examples which are not truly creative. Others, at a second level, may be based on existing prototypes known and studied by the student as he makes the insightful adaptations giving his creation some useful or pleasurable distinctiveness. But the highest level of creativity is original thinking or invention. In the case of technical subjects, these results may be obtained through scientific thinking or problem solving, or even through trial and error. In the creative arts, the product may be an original approach to expression in some appropriate medium such as writing, painting, or poetry. Chapter Six discusses criteria and procedures which may be used to evaluate and rate such creative projects.

## WORK EXPERIENCES AND INTERNSHIPS

Work experiences and internship opportunities have assumed added importance as means of independent learning in higher education. In many subject areas, they provide opportunities for students to gain the valuable skills and insights which cannot be had simply from studying books, listening to lectures, or working in laboratories. In professional education, for example, the internship fills the need for an advanced level of directed teaching. In this case, the intern (who has already graduated from college) teaches all or part of the day for pay as an employee of a cooperating school district. He is usually supervised by college personnel.

Similar arrangements are made also in other curriculum areas. In business administration, for example, students are sometimes assigned to work under college supervision for a period of time in purchasing, personnel, traffic, or merchandising departments of stores, factories, or in other kinds of business establishments.

## THE POSTLETHWAIT AUDIO-TUTORIAL PLAN[15]

The Audio-Tutorial Plan of instruction developed by S.N. Postlethwait and first applied to teaching botany at Purdue University provides a good example of the

[15] Adapted from S.N. Postlethwait, "An Audio-Tutorial Approach to Teaching Botany," in *New Media and College Teaching*, eds. James W. Thornton, Jr. and James W. Brown (Washington: National Education Association, 1968), p. 74.

**Figure 4-10.**
A booth is equipped with the materials for a week's study. These materials include physical items, such as plant specimens; projection items, such as 8 mm movies; an audio tape and printed materials, such as the text and study guide which each student brings with him.

**Figure 4-11.**
The student checks in at a vacant booth and is tutored through a sequence of learning activities by the voice of the senior instructor.

115

**Figure 4-12.**
The student is involved in a great variety of learning activities such as watching movies, reading from the text, examination of specimens, doing experiments and other appropriate studies integrated by the voice of the senior instructor.

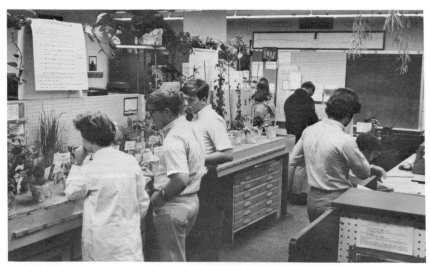

**Figure 4-13.**
Students may be requested to go to a central table for setting up experiments or making observations and may call upon the instructor on duty for assistance at any point in the study program.

**Figure 4-14.**
Expensive equipment or other items which are too bulky to be included in the booth are placed on a demonstration table.

**Figure 4-15.**
Some experiments may be conducted under greenhouse conditions and require collection of data over a period of several weeks.

**THE POSTLETHWAIT AUDIO-TUTORIAL PLAN AT PURDUE UNIVERSITY** *(continued)*

**Figure 4-16.**
Dr. Postlethwait listens to the student "teach" during a weekly quiz session.

several ways in which college instruction may be made more systematic along lines discussed in this chapter. Postlethwait began his plan (which has now been adopted and adapted by numerous institutions of higher education across the country) as an effort to adjust for the recognized diversity among his freshman botany students. The introductory course at Purdue involved approximately 380 students whose high school backgrounds in the subject were extremely varied. To assist those students with poor backgrounds to keep up with and succeed in the course, the instructor made a special supplementary lecture tape each week and placed it on reserve where those who needed to hear it might do so at their own convenience. It soon became evident that the student could also profit by having his textbook at hand while he listened to these lectures. Later, it seemed desirable to design the tapes in such a way as to capitalize on laboratory manual materials related to the same subjects. Still later, it became evident that it would be useful to add plants and experimental materials to complete a study kit.

Eventually, the tape content was changed from lecture to discussion on a teacher-student basis. The instructor's voice now tutors the student through a sequence of independent learning events carried out by students in laboratory carrels. Assignments, presented largely via the tape, involve such varied activities as reading from the text, doing an experiment, collecting and analyzing data, manipulating a microscope, watching time-lapse motion pictures, studying plant specimens, charts, diagrams, or photographs, and listening to brief lectures or discussions.

Success in using the first tapes also led to further refinements of the total audio-tutorial plan of which they are an important part. Present arrangements provide for the following: (1) a one-hour-per-week general session for all students, devoted largely to announcements, film showings, guest lecturers, and various course details; (2) supervised independent laboratory study sessions, from early morning to late at night, monitored by teaching assistants and carried out by students at individual study carrels equipped with tape playback or viewing equipment; (3) integrated quiz sessions, held weekly in sections of approximately eight students each, in which students teach other students by demonstrating mastery of the topic being studied; and (4) two independent miniature research projects—one provided in structured form, the other conducted as an experiment requiring from two to four hours to complete. Postlethwait concludes:

> The results of the audio-tutorial system have been positive from every point of view. Better instruction can be given with equal or less staff and space. Grades and student interest have improved at all levels. Costs are reduced for equivalent levels of instruction.[16]

## SUMMARY

The personal involvement of the student is essential if important and permanent learning is to occur. Chapter Four emphasizes this principle with practical examples, and discusses techniques for increasing the likelihood of such involvement. New developments as well as adaptations of traditional teaching styles are presented. The chapter reminds the beginning teacher of the variety of modes of presentation, so that he may select the ones most appropriate to the attainment of each of his course objectives. In addition, he will be aware of the value of a variety of activities in maintaining student interest.

Instructional formats discussed include variations in the purposes and utiliza-

---

[16] Postlethwait, *op. cit.*, p. 74.

tion of very large class groups, medium-sized groups, small groups, and individual instruction and independent study. A highly organized plan for directed independent study, the "audio-tutorial plan," was discussed at some length.

## RELATED READING

Caffrey, John, and Charles J. Mossman. *Computers on Campus.* Washington: American Council on Education, 1967.

Doll, Ronald C. (ed.). *Individualizing Instruction.* Washington: Association for Supervision and Curriculum Development, 1964.

Fuller, R. Buckminster. *Education Automation: Freeing the Scholar to Return to His Studies.* Carbondale, Ill.: Southern Illinois University Press, 1962.

Gage, N.L. *Handbook of Research on Teaching.* Washington: American Education Research Association, 1963.

Harnack, R. Victor, and Thorrel B. Fest. *Group Discussion.* New York: Appleton-Century-Crofts, 1964.

Jacobs, Paul I., Milton H. Maier, and Lawrence M. Stolurow. *A Guide to Evaluating Self-Instructional Programs.* New York: Holt, Rinehart and Winston, Inc., 1966.

Lange, Phil C. (ed.). *Programed Instruction.* Sixty-sixth Yearbook of the National Society for the Study of Education, Part II. Chicago: University of Chicago Press, 1967.

Mayhew, Lewis B. *Innovation in College Instruction.* Atlanta: Southern Regional Education Board, 1967.

Morphet, Edgar L., and David L. Jesser (eds.). *Planning for Effective Utilization of Technology in Education.* Denver: Designing Education for the Future Project, 1968.

Oettinger, Anthony G. *Run, Computer, Run: The Mythology of Educational Innovation.* Cambridge, Mass.: Harvard University Press, 1969.

Postlethwait, S.L., J. Novak, and H.T. Murray, Jr. *The Audio-Tutorial Approach to Learning* (2d ed.). Minneapolis: Burgess Publishing Co., 1969.

Rossi, Peter, and Bruce Biddle. *The New Media and Education.* Chicago: Aldine Publishing Co., 1966.

Scanlon, Robert G., and John O. Bolvin. *Individually Prescribed Instruction.* Philadelphia: Research for Better Schools, Inc., n.d.

Thornton, James W., Jr., and James W. Brown. *New Media and College Teaching.* Washington: National Education Association, 1968.

Williams, Harry. *Planning for Effective Resource Allocation in Universities.* Washington: American Council on Education, 1966.

# chapter five /
# INSTRUCTIONAL
# SERVICES AND
# RESOURCES / SELECTING INSTRUC-
TIONAL RESOURCES • MANAGING INSTRUCTIONAL RE-
SOURCE SERVICES • USING INSTRUCTIONAL RESOURCES •
SUMMARY • RELATED READINGS

The several basic aspects of systematic college teaching identified and described in Chapter Three were discussed in more detail in Chapter Four to show their relationships to alternative teaching modes or formats. In both cases "instructional resources" were referred to only briefly. Chapter Five examines several aspects of such resources: (1) a rationale to guide their selection and use by college professors; (2) typical logistical arrangements for managing their distribution and the professor's responsibilities with respect to those systems; and (3) instructional capabilities and recommended ways of using instructional resources that appear to have promise in higher education.

## SELECTING AND USING INSTRUCTIONAL RESOURCES

Instructors who adopt the systematic approach to teaching and learning need access to rich resources of instructional media, to equipment necessary to use those media, and to a logistical system to provide technical back-up services for them.

What is needed, at the outset, is a rationale to guide the selection and use of these resources to achieve the aims of college teaching. A first principle for such a rationale is that instructional resources should follow, not dictate, teaching aims. The most essential question is, "What should be taught or achieved?" It is important, but secondary, to ask, "What instructional resources are needed?" There is some danger of the instructor's losing sight of this fact when he surveys the ingenious electronic and mechanical aids to learning now appearing on the educational market. Today, more than ever before, it is essential to avoid the practice of stimulating the invention of educational devices and then of asking, "Now that we have them, how can they be used?" The first principle implies that it is uneconomical to use videotaping to achieve goals that are dependent solely upon communication through sound; if a programmed book with printed pictures can effectively present factual materials in science, it is not justifiable to use computers. Old purposes and practices may be outmoded, and innovations in instructional media may have exceptional value in encouraging instructors to analyze and improve their purposes, practices, and results with students. Nevertheless, it is unwise to try to do efficiently, through use of new media, what need not be done at all, or what could be done as well or better in less complicated, expensive, or time-consuming ways. This is not to argue for a status quo with regard to instructional media, devices, or techniques. But there are dangers in permitting any form of gadgetry to usurp educational decision making.

A second principle in the rationale for selecting (or developing) and using instructional resources is that one seldom finds existing media resources exactly fitting his course objectives, student characteristics, time requirements, teaching style, or fiscal capabilities; what is usually required is a more eclectic procedure for obtaining or developing resources. One such procedure[1] recommends the following steps:

State the behavioral objectives for the course or unit of instruction in the sequence in which they should be taught.

For each objective, identify the type of learning involved (concept learning, principle and "fact" learning, problem solving, skills, appreciations or attitudes).

Design a media program for each objective which lists the instructional events, identifies the characteristics of required stimuli, and states the media options which are possible and acceptable.

[1] Adapted from Leslie J. Briggs, et al., "A Procedure for Choosing Media for Instruction," in *Instructional Media: A Procedure for the Design of Multi-media Instruction* (Pittsburgh: American Institute for Research, 1967), pp. 28-29.

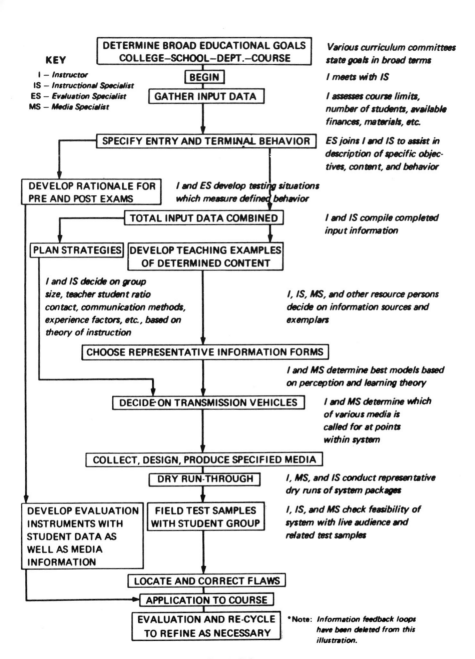

**Figure 5-1.**

A flow chart of procedures for analysis of instruction and implementation of newer media of communications. From John Barson, *Instructional Systems Development: A Demonstration and Evaluation Project.* USOE contract no. OE5-16-025 (East Lansing, Michigan: Michigan State University, 1967), p. 5.

Decide which of the available media techniques will be most effective in regard
to stimulus value, convenience in changing from one medium to another, and
economy for each of the objectives.

Write specifications for the preparation of media packages, all or parts of which
may already exist and others of which must be designed and produced
especially for the purpose.

Barson's flow chart[2] is a graphic representation of these selection and
development procedures.

A third principle in the selection and use of instructional resources is that
while there do appear to be critical differences in the capabilities of various
media for communicating certain kinds of learning experiences, no single medium is universally superior for all teaching purposes. Instructional materials are
sometimes classified in a way which manages to place each at some point on a
hypothetical continuum from abstract to concrete. When this is done, the
concrete items are sometimes mistakenly considered to be in some way better
than abstract items in the list. It is more accurate, of course, to regard each type
of instructional material as having some special (but not necessarily unique)
advantages and potentialities for teaching. It is helpful, too, to remind oneself
that there will be occasions when the best materials may be quite abstract (as,
for example, the words of an absorbing discussion), and that there will be other
occasions when different purposes will be served more effectively by a measure
of concreteness (such as a well-chosen film, a demonstration, a laboratory
experiment, or a visit to a slum area). Instructional value depends on the
adaptation of resources to the educational purposes for which they are used.

A fourth principle in selecting and using instructional resources is that
although considerable time and effort are needed to develop effective teaching
applications of media resources, results are often worth it. In higher education,
as elsewhere, it frequently seems easier to continue doing things as they have
always been done and to leave experimentation to others. It is understandable
that there is sometimes a reluctance to try new ways of teaching in colleges and
universities. College instructors do not wish to abandon practices which have
proved useful and particularly not for alternative practices in which they are
unskilled or which students themselves may dislike because of their unfamiliari-

[2]From John Barson, *Instructional Systems Development: A Demonstration and Evaluation
Project.* USOE contract no. OE5-16-025 (East Lansing, Michigan: Michigan State University, 1967), p. 00.

ty. College instructors are often reluctant to surrender some of their freedom of operation to other individuals or organizations on whom they must thenceforth depend. Some newer teaching media (as, for example, films and television) do require electronic equipment and, frequently, the services of a technician or projectionist. They also require dependence to some extent on an external organization to ensure that all scheduling details are properly managed and that the right materials appear in the right places under proper physical conditions. Things can and sometimes do go wrong at these junctures. And when they do, instructors lose face as well as confidence in the system no matter where the fault lies.

But if college teaching is to be improved, it must be studied continuously; creative, experimental approaches to teaching must be tried, evaluated, improved, and tried again. The everyday management of classroom activities must be seen as being filled with opportunities for testing one's ideas about teaching— for evaluating the efficacy of varied presentations, of student activities, and of other facets of student learning.

A fifth point in the rationale is that there are many different and acceptable ways of using instructional resources. Numerous research studies of instructional resources compare one pattern of use with another. Patterns investigated have included a variety such as the use of films alone (without instructor participation), the cross-media approach (involving interrelated uses of different kinds of materials), the extent and roles of instructor participation in the uses of materials (with or without introductions and goal setting versus formal goal setting, for example), or the relative contributions to learning derived from student participation and activity as materials are presented versus absence of such participation. Results of these and similar studies show that some use patterns are superior to others for certain purposes and under certain circumstances. But it is not surprising to find that, as with so many other complex aspects of teaching, no single method is universally superior.

Use of teaching resources is actually conditioned by many factors, no one of which the instructor may ignore. For example, he may introduce a film formally and stress specific points for students to notice; or he may show it without any introductory comment whatsoever. In either instance the important element is the specific purpose of the showing. In the first case, he may seek to stimulate orderly, searching observation of a particularly detailed film action; in the second, he may hope only for a kind of emotional involvement which a formal introduction would spoil.

A sixth point is that instructional resources do not replace college instructors; they extend and supplement their capabilities and permit them to perform differently while making their own unique contributions. Experience shows that some teaching resources (dial access listening facilities, for example) are capable of relieving instructors of the need for customary lectures, thus freeing time for other more important in-class or out-of-class activities. But it is difficult to conceive of the possibility of having college instruction taken over by mechanical or electronic devices without continued full and direct instructor participation. It seems far more realistic to regard teaching resources of all kinds (including both traditional and the newer technological aids) more as a means of improving an instructor's performance than of replacing him. In this view, television, programmed materials, books, slides, and recordings alike are media through which to present functionally varied learning experiences; they extend the instructor's powers and help to free him from performing in the monotonous and overworked role of lecturer.

A final point in the rationale is that no single instructor should expect to use all the instructional resources described here. Instead, he should analyze his own teaching aptitudes and requirements and give highest priority to improving his skills in using those which promise to contribute most toward the achievement of objectives important to his discipline. If through this process he neglects using some resources, this is no cause for concern. Although the instructor ought to give first attention to refining his skills in using resources with which he is already familiar before moving to those with which he is less familiar, he should adopt an experimental approach to determine more exactly the nature of contributions to be expected of the latter.

## MANAGING INSTRUCTIONAL RESOURCE SERVICES

College and university professors expect several institutional agencies to provide them with the instructional resources and services they need. At one time the library was the only such resource available in most colleges. But now, while the library is still of key importance, its role is being supplemented by other agencies which also influence the character and quality of college teaching. Chief among such agencies are the offices of (1) academic planning, staff development, and evaluation; (2) audiovisual or educational media services; and (3) instructional

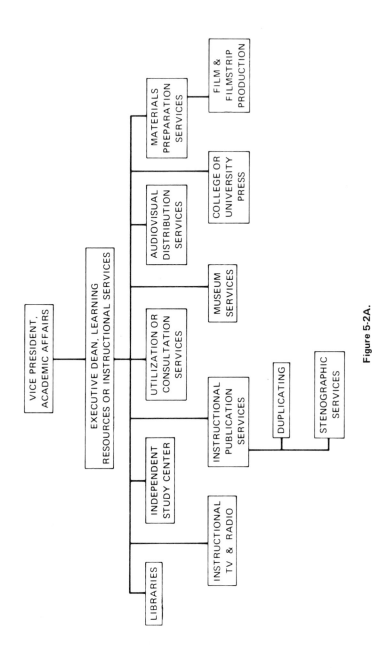

**Figure 5-2A.**

Instructional resource services. From Fred F. Harcleroad (ed.), *Learning Resources for Colleges and Universities* (Hayward, California: California State College, 1964), p. 20.

127

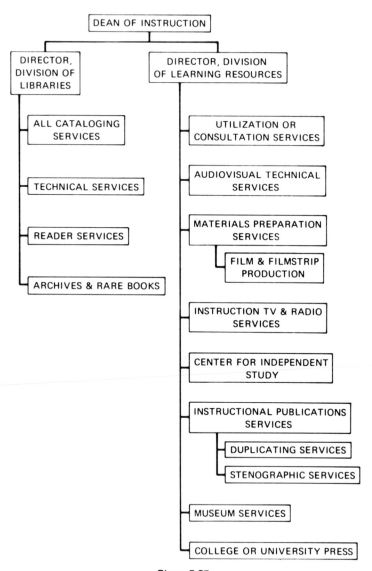

**Figure 5-2B.**
Instructional resource services. From Fred F. Harcleroad (ed.), *Learning Resources for Colleges and Universities* (Hayward, California: California State College, 1964), p. 21.

television services. In addition, still other kinds of learning resources and services are provided in most institutions through the college or university press, the bookstore, and such related agencies as the archives, scientific and anthropological museums, art museum, herbarium, arboretum, and others.

### ACADEMIC PLANNING AND DEVELOPMENT OFFICES

The complexities of managing and improving higher education have led recently to the establishment of institutional offices of academic planning to give needed direction to educational decision-making. Increased attention has also been given to processes of instructional innovation as institutions attempt to meet new challenges and to discharge new responsibilities as efficiently as possible. The need to allocate institutional resources equitably and efficiently to achieve new objectives has led, in turn, to a procedure known as program budgeting. Increasingly, planning, innovational programming, and budgeting are assigned to vice presidents for academic planning and development, offices of institutional research and development, centers for the improvement of college teaching, or similarly titled agencies.

Long-range planning is the essential first step toward general improvement of college teaching. Such planning involves clarification of the institution's nature and general purposes and precise specifications of functions and goals with respect to teaching, research, creative, and service activities for its clientele. Intermediate and long-range programming to achieve these goals requires attention to administrative structure, policies, and services for the institution as a whole and for each school or college, department, and program.

The relatively new term "program budgeting," which epitomizes the core requirement of such planning, seeks to estimate the economic costs and educational efficiencies of programs reflected in the institution's long-range plans. Three major aspects of program budgeting are usually described as: (1) planning—the establishment of long-range institutional goals and objectives; (2) programming—the application of specific elements of the long-range plan to shorter-range operations, such as those for an academic year; and (3) budgeting—allocating institutional resources including those usually reflected in the financial summary of its anticipated costs and support funds, to each important program element.

## INSTITUTIONAL LIBRARY SYSTEMS

College and university library systems comprise first lines of assistance to instructors in discharging teaching responsibilities. This point is stressed in an American Library Association statement on college library standards:[3]

> The college library should be the most important intellectual resource of the academic community. Its services ... should be geared to implement the purposes of the college's general program and to meet the specific educational objectives of the institution. Its collections should aim at presenting the heritage of Western and Eastern thought in all its richness, but should stress those particular areas which are central to the curriculum of the institution. No artificial barriers should separate the library from the classroom or the library staff from the teaching faculty. Beyond supporting the instructional program to the fullest extent, the library should endeavor to meet the legitimate demands of all its patrons, from the senior professor engaged in advanced research to the freshman just entering upon the threshold of higher learning, to stimulate and encourage the student to develop the lifelong habit of good reading, and to play its proper role in the community and in the wider realm of scholarship beyond the campus.

The college instructor has several responsibilities toward his institutional library. He is expected to familiarize himself with the organization and general rules of the library which apply to both students and faculty, details of which are often included in staff procedures manuals or special library brochures. The instructor must become acquainted with standards, procedures, and funds used in making new book or document purchase recommendations. The typical arrangement is to place responsibility for new library purchases in the hands of one or more individuals within a department who act as liaison with the library order department. The instructor is also expected to become familiar with library holdings in his field and to advise regularly through established channels on materials which should be purchased. Recommendations are also expected for weeding out obsolete or otherwise inappropriate materials in these same collections. Finally, cooperation is expected with the library's reserve book collections. The instructor should order items to be placed on reserve well in advance of his first class session.

[3] "Standards for College Libraries," *College and Research Libraries* 20(1959):274-280.

**Figure 5-3.**
The modern college or university learning resources center provides a variety of media and services to facilitate teaching and learning.

Faculty members frequently rely on inter-library loans to obtain materials not immediately available in collections at their own institutions. The American Library Association's Inter-Library Loan Code describes details of this service. Such loans are generally handled through libraries, not individuals. Ordinarily, libraries should not be asked to borrow materials from outside sources when they are owned locally. It is usually recommended that instructors require undergraduate students to undertake projects or studies for which adequate resource materials are available locally, with only occasional supplementary loans from other cooperating libraries.

**LEARNING RESOURCE CENTERS**

Various evolving programs of instruction in higher education (particularly those calling for increasingly individualized and independent study) place new and stimulating demands upon the professional personnel supplying instructional materials and technological services. The result has been increased attention to so-called non-book resources and services of the learning resources center, or the audiovisual facility.

Introduction of these expanded offerings recognizes the fact that knowledge may be made accessible in a variety of media, such as:

books
reference books, encyclopedias
magazines, newspapers
documents, clippings
duplicated materials
programmed, self-instructional materials (including computerized items)
films
videotape recordings
live television programs
radio programs
tape and disk recordings (audio)
photographs (paper prints)
drawings and paintings
slides and transparencies
filmstrips
microfilms, microcards, microfiches
stereographs
maps, globes
graphs, charts, diagrams
posters, cartoons
models, mockups, dioramas
collections, specimens, exhibits, displays

It has become increasingly common for colleges to unify the administration of learning resources and services, including library services, under a Director of Learning Resources. Yet many institutions continue separating traditional library services from new media services, placing each under its own director responsible to a chief academic administrative officer. It is less frequently the case that audiovisual services are provided independently of the library and through separate administrative channels.

Typical of non-book services to be expected from the modern college or university learning resources center are:

Consultation and assistance in choosing, designing, producing, and sequencing the use of various learning resources to achieve instructional objectives

Assistance of a technical nature in designing and constructing special facilities required for effective use of projected, audio, demonstration, or display learning resources

Maintaining collections of films, filmstrips, tape and disk recordings, large transparencies for loans to instructors, and ordering and financing rentals of similar items from other collections

Provision of technician assistance to handle projection or recording activities in the classroom

Procurement of items from outside sources for previewing or auditioning before recommending them for purchase

Maintenance, programming, and operation of electronic facilities (including the language laboratories and dial-access units)

Customized production services (8mm and 16mm films on local subjects, 2- by 2-inch slide reproductions, filmstrips, off-the-air, in-class, or studio audio tape recordings, and duplication or editing of them, videotape recordings and their duplication or editing, still photography, chart-making, model construction, display design and construction, duplication or printing services, and others).

## TELEVISION-RADIO BROADCASTING CENTERS

The number of higher education institutions involved in producing television and radio programs for instruction increases each year. Recent improvements in the quality of videotape equipment, coupled with drastic reductions of cost, have created new opportunities for using television in college teaching. The range of instructional applications of this medium is great. Specific examples of its uses and suggestions to instructors concerning ways of working with the medium, are given later in this chapter.

Radio broadcasting activities of colleges and universities are also increasing in scope and frequency, but usually with much less glamour and publicity than

**Figure 5-4.**
Most colleges and universities now provide staff and facilities for planning, producing, recording, and distributing television resources. (University of California, Santa Cruz)

those involved with television. Three forms of broadcasting are common: AM (amplitude modulation, on standard broadcast bands), FM (frequency modulation, on high frequency bands), and closed-circuit local-line broadcasting.

Exchanges of sound tapes between members of the National Association of Educational Broadcasters, carried on for many years, have resulted in the production of many programs used later as educational tapes for classroom teaching. The "Ways of Mankind" series in anthropology is one such example.

In carrying out all these activities, the campus television and radio broadcasting center usually works closely with faculty committees and individual faculty members, many of whom participate in program production or evaluation. Faculty members are usually expected to:

Become acquainted with services of the television and radio broadcasting center
    and its staff, to evaluate their possible relationship to classroom requirements
Participate, as appropriate, in the work of faculty committees maintaining
    advisory relationships with the center
Consider ways of participating in the production of radio or television programs
    for use by students or the public.

## OTHER INSTRUCTIONAL SERVICES

In institutions having college or university presses, additional special teaching resource services may be available to instructors. The institution's press is sometimes responsible for all types of duplicating services, including mimeographing, spirit duplicating, photocopying, and offset printing. University presses are of additional interest to the faculty because of their activities in publishing scholarly works (books, monographs, periodicals) which contribute to knowledge but which usually lack sufficiently wide appeal to attract commercial publishers.

College and university bookstores also provide various teaching resource services for the faculty. Chief among them is the sale of officially adopted textbooks. Most college bookstores are guided in textbook sale practices by the policies of the National Association of College Stores, developed cooperatively by its members. Faculty members are usually asked to make early decisions on textbook adoptions so as to permit the bookstore to canvass for used copies and to stock shelves before classes begin. Pricing practices for textbooks are fairly uniform among college bookstores everywhere. Typically, "Group 1" books (those to be used locally the following semester) are repurchased from students at 50 percent of the current new price. Books in "Group 2" (those not to be used locally the following semester but known to be in use at other institutions) are bought at lower prices.

Bookstores provide other instructional services for the faculty. They stock various laboratory or activity supply items; they handle the duplicating and binding of syllabi, manuals, or handbooks which have been developed by local instructors for use in their own classes; and they assist the faculty in obtaining books for personal use (complimentary copies of adopted textbooks, rare books, and similar items).

Other campus services and offices should be mentioned in a summary of institutional resources for teaching and learning. The anthropological and scientific collections of college or university museums must not be overlooked, for example, nor should those of the art museum. Institutional archives are often found to have special uses in some classes, as may the plant collections of the herbarium or aboretum.

But probably the greatest single instructional resource of any institution is its faculty; its members—all knowledgeable specialists in their own right—should be called upon to serve as resource persons to each other as circumstances permit.

## USING INSTRUCTIONAL RESOURCES

The college instructor's responsibilities include those of choosing and using the many instructional resources now provided through the various agencies of his institution. This section includes comments and suggestions about the choice and utilization of the following instructional resources: (1) textbooks, (2) supplementary printed materials, (3) programmed instructional materials, (4) television, (5) films, (6) sound and silent filmstrips, (7) still photographs, (8) 2- by 2-inch slides, (9) large transparencies, (10) microfilms, microcards, and microfiches, (11) charts and graphs, (12) chalkboards, (13) displays, (14) prerecorded tapes and disks, and (15) instructor- or student-made recordings.

### TEXTBOOKS

Textbooks have been described as uniquely American adaptations to the demands of mass education; they continue to occupy an important role in college teaching. They provide each student with a uniform body of basic information; they are often illustrated with clear diagrams, graphs, pictures, or maps—many in color. The combination of theory, research summaries, facts or principles, interpretive comments, thought questions, suggested learning assignments and activities, and lists of selected references provides an organized approach to the study of a subject.

Textbooks which have been officially selected for use in a particular college or university are said to have been adopted. The formality of this process varies with institutions. In some, the instructor may simply notify the bookstore of his intention to use a certain text in his class; in others, a change of text may require formal approval by the appropriate department head, dean, or faculty committee. Textbook adoption regulations exist to protect students (and the bookstore) against frequent or needless changes of texts with consequent loss of money. It is the responsibility of the instructor to learn and to abide by or change rules and regulations in effect in his institution. The faculty manual usually carries a complete statement about the matter.

Two publications will assist instructors in *selecting* textbooks for their classes, as follows:

*Textbooks in Print,* issued yearly, by R.R. Bowker Company, New York, indexed by author, title, and subject, with complete bibliographic data.

*Cumulative Book Index,* issued monthly by the H.W. Wilson Co., New York, with cumulations at regular intervals.

In deciding among several competing textbooks, the instructor must ask several important questions. The following are suggestive:

Does the textbook treat the major topics of the course with the required depth, detail, and sequence?

Is the textbook written by recognized experts in the field? Have the reviews been good?

Is its treatment sufficiently up to date? Are some topical treatments outdated by recent developments or omitted altogether?

Is its treatment sufficiently sophisticated for the students who will use it? Does it assume too little or too much background in the subject?

Does the treatment (content, emphasis, and interpretation) agree fundamentally with the point of view of the course instructor? This is to suggest that students should be spared the confusion of approaching the subject from one point of view in the text and of having the instructor present a quite opposite point of view in class. Differing points of view might better be presented in supplementary readings or other materials, discussed later in this section.

Is the textbook planned and written to facilitate student learning? Does it include appropriate graphics which illuminate ideas rather than decorate pages? Does it contain review and thought-question devices which are practical and helpful?

Is the book technically satisfactory? Is the type large enough? Does the book design (page size, columnar arrangement, illustration balance and size) contribute to communication of ideas? Is the book too long, too detailed, too short, too sketchy in treatment?

Is the textbook properly priced?

Answers to many of the foregoing questions may be obtained from the instructor's own inspection of the one or more textbooks considered for his course. He may also obtain help by (1) consulting colleagues who have used the book before him, (2) studying journal reviews, or (3) seeking the opinions of students who have either used the book with a previous class or who, because of their qualifications, have been asked to read and evaluate it. It should be pointed out, of course, that it will be unusual to find through these processes a single textbook which satisfies all criteria. Although the textbook eventually selected will no doubt be the one which comes closest to the specifications, it, too, may be lacking in one or more characteristics the instructor considers essential. Teaching with the book then becomes properly a process of adaptation to some of its shortcomings rather than an occasion for frequent tirades on the incompetence or ignorance of textbook authors. Although the tirades may relieve instructor tensions, they do little to help the student who has paid his money for the book.

Experienced college instructors have made several recommendations concerning ways of using textbooks:

Consider the textbook somewhat as a teaching assistant whose out-of-class presentations in print do not require restatement in class. Instead, supplement, elaborate on, interpret, or clarify its ideas in class.

Help students, especially freshmen, make effective use of the textbook as a study device. During early class sessions, discuss its organization and treatment of topics, suggest ways of studying it most systematically, emphasize the importance of the review, graphic, and index materials it contains.

Refer to and comment upon the textbook. Students are disconcerted to find that some instructors require the purchase of a textbook and then ignore it. Items drawn from the text are appropriate in tests.

Require students to study and to work with more than just the textbook for the course. The text usually provides an organized approach to the subject—but this should be thought of as a point of departure for numerous forays into other materials, including original sources, periodicals, reference books, or supplementary books. Contrasting facts, points of view, or conclusions will help students to learn to think for themselves rather than to rely on others to do it for them.

Instructors are also expected to become familiar with institutional regulations pertaining to the preparation of instructional material for sale to students. It is commonly a requirement that all such items must meet certain local criteria before such arrangements may be made.

## SUPPLEMENTARY PRINTED MATERIALS

In recommending reference books and periodicals for library purchases, the instructor will find several bibliographic publications useful. In addition, catalogs of educational publishers can serve to keep him informed of current publications in his own discipline. The most widely used *bibliographic aids* are the following:

*American Book Publishing Record*, published yearly. A record of American book production for the year, as cataloged by the Library of Congress.

*Bibliographic Index,* issued semiannually by the H.W. Wilson Company, New York. A bibliography of bibliographies on a wide variety of subjects.

*Book Review Digest*, issued monthly except July, by the H.W. Wilson Company. Reviews approximately four thousand books each year (by author). Includes cumulative subject and title indexes in alphabetical order.

*Book Review Index,* issued bimonthly, with yearly cumulations, by Gale Research Company. Index reviews approximately 220 scholarly periodicals and lists reviews of some 40 thousand books annually.

*Booklist-Subscription Books Bulletin,* issued by the American Library Association. A buying guide for librarians and others, listing books in all classes by Dewey and Library of Congress systems.

*Books for College Libraries,* edited by M.J. Voigt, published by American Library Association. Lists approximately 53 thousand titles based on initial selections made for new campuses of the University of California, 1967. 1,056 pages.

*Books for Junior Colleges,* published by the American Library Association, listing approximately four thousand books in print, films, periodicals, and filmstrips on the basis of usefulness in junior college instruction, selected under the sponsorship of the American Association of Junior Colleges, 1954. 321 pages.

*Books in Print,* issued annually by R.R. Bowker Company, New York, listing in one volume reprints of catalogs issued by various publishers. Another volume, *Subject Guide to Books in Print,* indexes all titles in the former volume according to their subjects.

*Cumulative Book Index,* issued monthly by the H.W. Wilson Company, with cumulations at regular intervals, listing all books in English excepting government publications.

*Paperbound Books in Print,* issued semiannually by R.R. Bowker Company, New York, listing approximately six thousand inexpensive paperback reprints and originals, with subject guide.

Winchell, Constance: *Guide to Reference Works,* American Library Association, Chicago. Revised annually. A comprehensive guide to various reference works with emphasis upon those to be found in college and university libraries.

Additional reference aids which will be found useful in *locating articles* appearing in periodicals include:

*Education Index,* issued monthly except July and August, by the H.W. Wilson Company, indexing most references to education in all important American sources (periodical and other) and some British ones. Includes numerous headings dealing with higher education.

*Social Sciences and Humanities Index,* formerly the *International Index to Periodicals.* Issued quarterly, by H.W. Wilson Company, indexing principally journals devoted to social sciences and humanities.

*Reader's Guide to Periodical Literature,* issued twenty-two times yearly, with biennial, annual, and other cumulative issues, by H.W. Wilson Company, including reference citations for approximately 120 selected periodicals of general interest.

Reference aids which will be found helpful in locating *publication data* for various United States and foreign periodicals include:

*America's Educational Press: A Classified List of Educational Periodicals Issued in the United States Together with an International List of Educational Periodicals,* issued in odd years by the Educational Press Association of America, Washington, D.C. Provides names, addresses, prices, circulation figures, and related data.

*Directory of Newspapers and Periodicals,* issued annually by N.W. Ayer and Son, Philadelphia, listing approximately twenty thousand newspapers, magazines, and other publications.

*New Serial Titles,* issued quarterly with annual cumulative volumes by R.R. Bowker Company. Lists new periodical titles, title changes, and discontinuations.

Ulrich, Carolyn F.: *Periodicals Directory: A Classified Guide to a Selected List of Current Periodicals, Foreign and Domestic,* issued approximately each three years, by R.R. Bowker Company, New York, containing classified listing of periodicals.

*Union List of Serials,* issued by the H.W. Wilson Company, New York.

*Writer's Market,* issued annually (in some years semiannually) by Writer's Digest Publishing Company, Cincinnati, Ohio, and useful as a checklist and for obtaining names, addresses, and publication data on hundreds of magazines.

### PROGRAMMED INSTRUCTIONAL MATERIALS

The use of programmed approaches to college instruction presents special problems:

If programmed materials are to be used, programs will need to be found or produced locally that meet one's expectations and specifications.

Programs requiring nonportable machines (as opposed to book types or individual, low-cost machines which can be carried by the user) will require special rooms; someone must be responsible for loading and maintaining machines, and reclaiming and analyzing residual answer sheets. Programmed books have the advantages of portability, flexibility, low cost, and individualization.

The instructor who gives programmed assignments to students must consider the changes this action is likely to require in the usual patterns of in-class and out-of-class activities. Instructors sometimes find that they are devoting more time in class to discussion of misunderstandings arising from out-of-class study of programmed materials and less time to lecturing or other instructor-presentation techniques.

Instruction must be given students in how to use programmed materials and equipment. Such skills and understandings cannot be assumed.

In developing programmed instructional systems, college instructors will usually seek the expert assistance of learning resource or other center specialists. The following are recommended steps of the process:[4]

*Develop, write down, and share with the students the appropriate instructional objectives for the program.* Good objectives will make clear to students how they will be changed by the learning experiences provided—what they will know, what they will be able to do, how they will feel as a result of them. The objectives will also specify the conditions of achievement and the expected level of proficiency.

*Specify the criterion tests to be used.* These tests should be tied very closely to the original objectives for the instruction provided. Posttests should show clearly the level of proficiency attained by students; comparison of posttest with pretest scores will provide an estimate of the degree to which students changed (improved) as a result of instruction.

*Write the program.* The program itself should comprise a *plan* based on the foregoing procedures that will guide and sequence the instruction and thus lead toward expected behavioral changes. A major task at this stage is to select (or produce) a variety of appropriate learning experiences. These experiences may be provided through programmed or traditionally-prepared text materials, instructor lectures, discussions, projected or audio materials, or other means.

*Use and evaluate the success of the program.* Compare the final student performance with criterion measures suggested as suitable for each important objective, under the circumstances and within prescribed levels of acceptability.

*Rework and attempt to improve the program in anticipation of its next use.* Such reworking is expected to be a continuous process.

## TELEVISION

Several claims made for the use of television in higher education, are substantiated by research and experience. Televised instruction permits the well-

---

[4] Adapted from James W. Brown, R.B. Lewis, and F.F. Harcleroad, *A V Instruction: Media and Methods* (New York: McGraw-Hill, 1969), pp. 116-117.

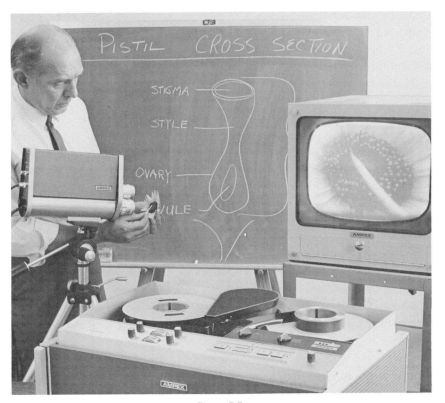

**Figure 5-5.**
The image magnification television camera and portable tape recorder provide unique tools for presenting appropriately timed, edited, and dramatically understandable learning experiences. (Ampex Corporation)

qualified instructor to reach more students at one time than could normally be accommodated in the classroom. Televised procedures can reduce unit costs and keep tuition fees within reach of more students than would otherwise be possible. This approach makes feasible the concentration of effort upon one fairly brief instructional presentation (determining objectives, planning the approach, developing visual or audio materials to illustrate points, practicing delivery, evaluating results).

Additional claims with regard to the effectiveness of television as an instructional medium, as compared with other more traditional forms of instruction are somewhat less convincing. But Pennsylvania State University's early studies of television teaching (fairly typical of others of a similar nature that have been conducted since) showed that college students do as well on regularly prepared tests by taking courses over television as by taking them in small groups with direct personal contact with professors.[5]

In a more recent survey of televised instruction in higher education,[6] the following common uses of the medium were identified:

As a substitute for "live" professor presentations in an auditorium. With this use, one or two cameras are focused on the professor as he lectures; sometimes he addresses himself solely to the camera. The televised event may be sent live to other locations on campus, or videotaped and stored for a variety of other uses. Professors sometimes use tapes as stand-ins for themselves when they must be absent or as "rerun" opportunities for students.

As an image-magnifier to enlarge realia, documents, pictures, or microscopic slides so they may be viewed on classroom (or even remote) monitors.

As a means of transmitting instructional programs (which may only be replications of regular classroom events) to remote locations where it is not possible or economically feasible to staff a course, or to present a specific contribution of some noted lecture-demonstrator. Inter-institutional exchanges of televised instructional programs are sometimes arranged in this manner.

As a means of improving instruction by videotaping short demonstrations, or bringing together on one continuous tape a number of instructional resources (documentary film clips, visual records of field trips, other televised programs, slides, and similar items), and of using such materials at strategic times during class sessions. Problems associated with time-consuming, inconveniently scheduled, or expensive learning experiences may be overcome in this way.

To permit large numbers of individuals to observe classroom activities, interviews, or similar events without obtruding their presence and perhaps invalidating the experiences.

To permit repeated and conveniently timed observations of the same event (thus, to some extent, controlling and standardizing its impact).

To facilitate self-observation and study—for students or professors.

---

[5]C.R. Carpenter, *College Teaching by Television* (Washington: American Council on Education, 1958), p. 16.

[6]Adapted from James W. Thornton, Jr. and James W. Brown, *New Media and College Teaching* (Washington: National Education Association, 1968), pp. 22-23.

To provide opportunities for students to make creative use of the medium in preparing documentary or dramatized presentations as class assignments.

Experience usually shows that the role of the professors is changed in one or more ways by his participation in televised instruction. He must:

*Learn to function as a member of a production team.* This must be done whether he appears alone or as one of several instructors assisted by other professional and technical coworkers (directors, writers, cameramen, sound, light, and boommen). Teaching by means of television is a new technique with which most instructors learn to work satisfactorily.

*Learn to expect and to adapt to changes in ways of interacting with students and professional colleagues.* The professor who teaches several hundred students at a time on a closed-circuit network appears via screens and loudspeakers all over the campus. Much of his success will depend on his ability to project his personality in a forceful, interesting manner and upon his capacity to use the slim feedback cues (student and section leader comments, written statements or questions, instantaneous telephone line question feedback devices, and others) to guide future presentations. Conferences with students and section leaders will thus be of primary importance in determining changes and improvements needed in his presentations. With some instructors, the capacity to respond to advice and criticism without rancor may be difficult to develop. The television instructor, additionally, will often need to adjust his ways of relating to students when they are asked to assume increased responsibilities for their own education.

*Learn to live in the more or less public gaze.* The instructor who teaches on television soon learns that he is being subjected to the sometimes mercilessly critical view of a largely unseen audience. This is the case whether the program is released live on closed-circuit, via open-circuit broadcast facilities, or on tape for later uses. Traditionally, instructors have had the privilege of teaching in private (with the exception of occasional visits from department heads or senior colleagues during pretenure days). There has always seemed to be some sanctity attached to one's administering the professorial rites; but the TV camera appears to some to be poised to invade this privacy. Up to now, however, problems raised by this situation have been handled largely by means of the polite refusal. The instructor who has not wanted to teach on television has been given the privilege of declining the honor. Whether circumstances will continue this permissiveness in the future remains to be seen.

*Learn to fill new roles in teaching.* There is little doubt that the instructor who participates in televised teaching will experience some role changes related to specialization. For example, he may function as the individual in charge of a single section of students who receive their lecture presentations from a major professor in a studio some distance away. What the instructor does in this case is certain to be different from what professors have been known to do under the ordinary circumstances of teaching. Probably for some time to come, students as well as professors will be aware of this difference, and both will need to adjust to it. The section instructor in particular will need to learn new ways of relating his work to that of the professor in charge, and of functioning as a discussant of the ideas presented.

*Consider the economics of the "automated" professor.* Televised instruction introduces a number of problems with respect to providing fair and adequate compensation to professors involved. Special complications are introduced when programs are made into videotapes or films for reuse at other times or places or when they are transmitted simultaneously for multiple uses in other institutions.

### FILMS

Motion picture films have myriad uses in higher education. They are capable of enlarging, slowing down, or speeding up action, visualizing the unobservable (through dramatizations or documentary presentations), heightening interest (through various dramatic effects), and juxtaposing experiences (through cutting and editing techniques) for emphasis and clarification. Each of these potentialities has useful applications in college and university teaching.

Several developments in the film medium have increased opportunities for its use in higher education. Recent improvements in film quality, for example, now make 8mm screen images in color the approximate equal of 16mm images of a few years ago. Additionally, 8mm cartridge-type sound projectors (some using film to which the sound track has been added with a material similar to that used in surfacing recording tape) are on the market. The result of these developments is that 8mm sound motion pictures may now be produced quite inexpensively; they may be projected with minimum technical difficulty under classroom conditions which until a few years ago would have required at least the 16mm size.

Increasing uses of cartridged 8mm sound and silent films are also being made in independent study situations, usually within carrels installed in the library or audiovisual or learning resources center.

Research with regard to contributions of films to teaching has implications for higher education. As might be expected, films have been found useful in teaching facts; on some occasions they have been found to be almost as effective in teaching these facts alone as were instructors with their usual methods of teaching. The effectiveness of films has also been established in aiding the teaching of certain perceptual-motor skills, such as those related to industrial operations, physical education, and armed services activities. Studies of film use have suggested their utility in teaching concepts, as opposed to strictly factual learning. They have also been shown to be helpful in modifying motivations, interests, attitudes, and opinions.

Several recommended practices in utilizing films are supported generally by research:[7] To enhance film learning, the instructor should:

*Be familiar with the film.* Advance preview is recommended. Study the accompanying film guide (copies of which generally may be purchased from film producers). Some audiovisual or learning resource centers maintain film title files containing previous user comments and evaluations, film reviews, and other materials in developing plans for utilizing films. Take notes during the preview, giving special attention to the film's organization, key points of emphasis, and possible issues and ideas around which to focus its later introduction and post-showing discussion.

*Develop a favorable student motivational set for seeing or studying the film.* Introduce the film and indicate fairly specifically what students are expected to learn from it. Instructors often (1) state the film title, (2) give a brief resumé of its points of emphasis and state its relationship to the current work of the class, (3) state (or write on the board) the problems to which answers will be sought in the film showing, (4) discuss the meaning of key terms to provide better

---

[7]For further information, see Charles F. Hoban, "The Usable Residue of Educational Film Research," in *New Teaching Aids for the American Classroom* (Stanford, California: Institute for Communication Research, 1960), pp. 95-115.

communication, and (5) indicate the nature of the follow-up activities to be conducted after the film showing (test, discussion, application, or other).

*Stimulate appropriate student participation during the film showing.* It is important that students participate mentally (and sometimes verbally or physically) while seeing films. In most cases films will be shown without interruption. But each student should be stimulated to participate mentally by giving special attention to content in relation to the original "points to look for." If there are stops for interspersed practice of skills demonstrated, students should be encouraged to verbalize film content. Note-taking during skill-film showings usually is not recommended; it may help with other types of films.

*Conduct suitable follow-up activities.* These may include the discussion of original points assigned for the viewing attention of students. It may also include a point-by-point review of the film essentials, with brief analytical discussion of each. In the case of dramatized films, there may be an evaluation of the characterizations of persons in leading roles. Tests, too, are sometimes given as means of checking student comprehension. Immediate scoring of brief, objective tests sometimes serves as the means of organizing the postshowing film discussion. With skill films, opportunities should be given for immediate applications of the operations demonstrated. Reshowing of all or portions of films is recommended when necessary to clarify points, to correct misinformation, or to provide further practice.

It is frequently appropriate, of course, to vary some of the approaches to film utilization just described. Films need not always be shown in their entirety, for example; they may be shown only to some crucial point and stopped. Class members may then be asked to discuss or to write a resolution of the action or drama from that point on. Upon completion of this assignment, the rest of the film may be shown and compared with the way the students resolved it. Sound films may also be shown as silent films—with the sound turned off—while the instructor narrates, questions, or explains in his own words and in ways which have particular meaning to his class.

Reference aids useful in helping instructors to obtain descriptions of content, sources, purchase or rental costs, running times, production dates, and similar information about films, include the following:

*Index to 16mm Educational Films,* available from the R.R. Bowker Company, 1180 Avenue of the Americas, New York, New York 10036. An alphabetical, by film title, directory providing key information for more than 30,000 educational and documentary films.

*Index to 8mm Educational Motion Picture Cartridges,* also available from R.R. Bowker Company, cataloging some nine thousand 8mm motion picture cartridge titles.

*Bluebook of Audiovisual Materials,* issued annually by the Audiovisual Guide and Educational Screen Magazine, Chicago, listing recently produced films of educational value.

Issues of *Audiovisual Instruction,* the official magazine of the Association for Educational Communications and Technology, 1201 Sixteenth Street, N.W., Washington, D.C. 20036.

Additional valuable information may be obtained from the college library or audiovisual or learning resources center. Journals of various learned societies of one's professional associations often carry excellent film reviews oriented toward the problems of college instruction.

### SOUND AND SILENT FILMSTRIPS

35mm filmstrips—silent (with printed titles or captions) or sound (with accompanying tape or disk), in black and white or color are useful in college instruction. The typical filmstrip contains anywhere from twenty to one hundred frames, or individual pictures, on from two to six feet of 35mm film. Offerings of well-planned filmstrips have increased considerably within the past few years, so much so that there is now at least some coverage for most curriculum topics. The number applicable to the needs of higher education has increased proportionately.

Most filmstrips are silent, and plans for their utilization must recognize this fact. Because only a few aspects of filmstrip utilization differ in any important particulars from that of film utilization, only these will be mentioned, as follows:

*Stand at the front of the room,* preferably near the screen, and have the projection handled by a member of the class or by an outside projectionist.

This procedure enables the instructor to maintain contact with the class and to point out picture details, as appropriate.

*Read the printed captions aloud as the filmstrip is projected.* The instructor may do this, or one or more students may be asked to do it. The instructor may inject questions and interpretive comments from time to time.

*Concentrate on talking about what appears on the screen.* To talk about something else, while the screen image remains for all to see, is likely to be confusing.

*Move along at a proper pace.* Do not lose attention by permitting individual frames to remain on screen for too long a time.

*Back up, skip, use hand flash techniques.* Simply because frames of a filmstrip are arranged sequentially, it does not follow that the instructor cannot vary the order of their use. With a little practice, the operator can learn to skip frames (hand over lens, counting the frame clicks), back up (with same procedures), or test class comprehension by short flash exposures (hand over lens) of appropriate frames.

Useful information sources concerning filmstrips include the following:

*Index to 35mm Educational Filmstrips,* available from R.R. Bowker Company, 1180 Avenue of the Americas, New York, New York, 10036. Titles, number of frames, whether silent or sound, date of release, and other data are provided.

Catalogs of various filmstrip producers and files of the college library or audiovisual or learning resources center.

### STILL PHOTOGRAPHS

Still photographs are also useful tools for a variety of purposes in college teaching. For small-group purposes they may be held up for all to see and talk about; in larger groups they may be placed in an opaque projector, or handed around in sequence after first being talked about by the instructor. Such photographs, combined with titles and captions, are also useful for display boards.

Instructor-made still photographs are being used more widely as a result of improved Polaroid Land camera developments. This unit provides a particularly helpful tool for recording field trip details for later study and analysis by the class.

**Figure 5-6.**
The modern 35mm reflex camera permits even the inexpert person to produce small transparencies which often have significant impact in teaching.

## 2- BY 2-INCH SLIDES

Slides in the 2- by 2-inch format (or 2¼- by 2¼-inch or 3¼- by 4-inch) are commonly used in college and university teaching. They are, in fact, more widely used than most of the other tools discussed so far, with the possible exception of films. Their advantages are numerous: They may be developed rather inexpensively by the instructor or by the staff of the local audiovisual center, to meet local teaching requirements; they may be edited, revised, and brought up to date as new needs dictate; they are capable of presenting the reality of full color; and they can be produced with minimum equipment of the type many instructors already own and know how to use.

The audiovisual center staff is usually able to provide expert assistance to instructors who wish to learn how to plan and photograph slides. In some cases, the center also furnishes raw film and processing when photographs are for official instructional or research purposes.[8]

[8]For further information about the production of 2- by 2-inch slide materials for instruction, see James W. Brown, et al., *AV Instruction: Media and Methods* (McGraw-Hill Book Company, Inc., New York, 1969), pp. 468-473.

A few suggestions for instructors intending to produce their own slide units follow:

*Think through the instructional goals* intended to be served by the slide unit.

*Start with a plan* that translates these goals into an organized set of pictures, each contributing its part to the message. The plan should describe verbally the content of each proposed picture (shooting script).

*Include enough close-ups* to give viewers the sense of detail which is usually needed with visual presentations in slide form.

*Shoot a sufficient number of pictures* to provide the between-picture continuity needed to give the viewer the complete story. "Step pictures" are a help in this connection—pictures which lead gradually, through recognizable steps, from the beginning to the end of some process.

*Strive for interesting and useful composition* which guides the viewer to a center of interest and communicates the important picture elements intended.

*Strive for technical excellence*—correct exposure, camera steadiness, balance of light and shadow, and so on.

*Edit courageously,* eliminating pictures which do not belong, which are poorly exposed, which duplicate.

*Try out the finished product* and rearrange, reshoot, and improve, as necessary.

## LARGE TRANSPARENCIES

Large transparencies, especially useful in college teaching, are usually developed in the 10- by 10-inch (overall dimensions) format for use in the overhead projector. Because of its wattage and large optical system, this machine is capable of projecting readable large screen images with room lights on. A further advantage of this medium is that it permits the instructor to handle his own projection while facing the class and maintaining eye contact from the front of the room. At any time, he may use a pencil to point out features of the slide he wishes the class to study.

Chance, at the University of Texas, compared the instructional effectiveness of projected overhead transparencies and instructor-made chalkboard illustrations in engineering drawing classes.[9] He concluded that approximately fifteen

[9]Clayton W. Chance, *Experimentation in the Adaptation of the Overhead Projector Utilizing 200 Transparencies and 800 Overlays in Teaching Engineering Descriptive Geometry Curricula* (Austin: The University of Texas, 1960).

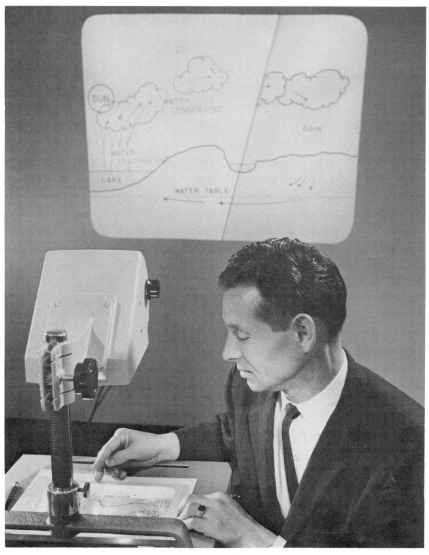

**Figure 5-7.**
Large transparencies may be projected satisfactorily under ordinarily difficult lighting conditions, with the instructor facing the class.

minutes of each sixty-minute period could be saved by use of the transparency as compared with the chalkboard method. Further, he found no significant difference in student drawing proficiencies, significantly superior grades in the transparency group, a higher degree of student attentiveness in the transparency group (as measured by number of questions asked), and greater numbers of instructors and students favoring use of the transparency rather than the chalkboard.

A variety of processes are used in producing transparencies for the overhead projector. Three machine types are known by the trade names of Ozalid, Apeco, and Thermofax. Hand-drawn slides, too, are an important teaching resource for some classes. Color may be used in either machine-produced or hand-drawn transparencies. The audiovisual center production staff will usually provide assistance with the development of both items.

For further data concerning characteristics and availabilities of prepared large transparencies, consult *Index to Overhead Transparencies*, available from R.R. Bowker Company, 1180 Avenue of the Americas, New York, New York, 10036.

### MICROFILMS, MICROCARDS, AND MICROFICHES

It is increasingly common for scholars to have access to many rare or otherwise expensive materials in microfilm or microcard form. College and university libraries everywhere are likely to have in their collections (or they can obtain them) hundreds and sometimes thousands of microfilms or microcards for titles which would ordinarily be beyond their reach. And it is often easier to borrow from other libraries items which are in microfilm form than to obtain them in printed or original forms. Out-of-print books, too, are sometimes made available by publishers in this way.

One particularly useful source of information about microfilms is the *Union List of Microfilms*, issued occasionally by J.W. Edwards, Publisher, Inc., Ann Arbor, Michigan. It lists alphabetically thousands of titles in microfilm form owned by more than two hundred important libraries in the United States. Another publication of specialized use is *A Guide to the Microfilm Collection of Early State Records*, issued in 1950 by the Library of Congress.

*Microfiche* means "miniature index card." Modern-day microfiche materials are being made available through ERIC (Educational Research Information Centers) operated through grants from the U.S. Office of Education, as well as other sources. Through the services of such units, educators and others may purchase (for approximately 10 cents) transparent film sheets averaging sixty pages of book copy. College and university libraries have the equipment that permits these transparencies to be read as projected enlargements on a special reader screen, or printed as paper copies in the original size.

### CHARTS AND GRAPHS

Various forms of charts and graphs have also been found to have special values in college teaching. Some instructors prefer charts to transparencies for materials they wish to show to small groups because of the ease with which they may be used; the room need not be darkened, equipment is not needed, and multiple or repeated exposures of charts may be made, as desired.

In developing chart materials for his classes, the instructor may usually count on assistance from the audiovisual center. The following suggestions should be considered:

Adopt a large enough size for charts to enable students to read them from all parts of the room. A 20- by 30-inch chart is usually considered minimal in such cases; they may be much larger and often should be. It is a good plan to make a preliminary test of one or more charts in the room in which they will be used.

Make all charts to the same uniform size, preferably, whether or not each particular subject may require it. Make them all vertical or horizontal; do not mix them.

Give each chart a clear and simple title; indicate the basis for scale or measurements; indicate sources of data.

Choose the proper graph type for presenting statistical data comparisons: bar, line, pictograph, circle, or pie.[10]

Use color to heighten interest and to facilitate communication.

Keep charts simple both with respect to facts or ideas communicated and their manner of presentation. It is better to divide complex materials into more than one chart rather than to crowd or confuse with too much.

[10] A particularly valuable reference for guiding the preparation of chart and graph materials is James E. Parker, *Communicating Quantitative Data: Graphs* (Durham, N.C.: North Carolina College Bookstore, 1960).

## CHALKBOARDS

The chalkboard is often regarded as the instructor's chief tool for communicating and clarifying ideas. A few general pointers may improve its utilization:

Use the chalkboard to supplement and reinforce other parts of the presentation, discussion, or demonstration. As key terms are mentioned, write them on the board, pronounce them, define them, and give examples to clarify their meanings and importance.

Write or print large enough and heavily enough to allow students to read clearly from all parts of the room. Experiment by attempting to read various writing specimens from different parts of the room. Practice printing so that it can be done quickly and fairly uniformly.

Use colored chalks (as well as capital letters, lower case printing, or freehand writing) to emphasize relationships and relative importance of items in chalkboard illustrations.

Use only standard abbreviations; write out labels and terms in full.

Add items to the chalkboard as they are introduced in the presentation. If items are placed on the chalkboard ahead of class, keep them covered, if possible, until they are needed. In-class sketching may be facilitated by drawing before class light outlines which are filled in more heavily at the appropriate time during the class hour. Outline patterns or templates may also be used.

Start at the left and work to the right of the board, in columns, somewhat in the proportions of 8½- by 11-inch paper. Use ruled lines or the natural divisions of the board to indicate "sheets."

Stand aside so that students may see what is written on the board.

Talk to the class, not to the board.

Reduce clutter and confusion by erasing unneeded items promptly. At the end of the period, leave the board clean and ready for use by following instructors.

## DISPLAYS

Various display forms of interest to college and university instructors should be considered at least briefly in this discussion of teaching resources. These displays include bulletin boards, feltboards (or magnetic boards), and exhibits. Each has special applications to classroom teaching. The feltboard is a particular help in illustrating ideas for repetitive presentations, such as with multiple sections of the same course taught during any semester. Bulletin boards and exhibits are appropriate means of highlighting certain aspects of a course as, for example, a display of recommended books (brought together with the help of the library staff) or an exhibit of student products developed in the course (paintings, outlines, organizational charts). Student committees are often assigned responsibilities for developing such displays as supplements to student reports or discussions.

## PRERECORDED TAPES AND DISKS

Within recent years, offerings of prerecorded tapes and disks (primarily of the latter) have become so numerous, so varied, and of such high quality that they must now be regarded as some of the most important of the many teaching resources available to college and university instructors. The college learning resources or audiovisual center and the library are the usual sources of such materials on the campus. Included in their collections will be found recordings of important speeches of the past and recent past, musical performances ranging from symphonic to exotic, radio programs of lasting interest, interviews, readings of poetry, dramatizations, and special purpose recordings (such as those of frogs or birds in various dithers, the Morse code, foreign language exercises, and others).

A principal source of prerecorded nonmusical tapes is maintained by the Audiovisual Center, University of Colorado, Boulder, Colorado, which is identified with the National Tape Recording Project of the Association for Educational Communications and Technology.[11]

In teaching a full class with prerecorded nonmusical tapes or disks, the following suggestions are given:

*Audition the material to become familiar with it.* Again, as with films and visual materials used in teaching, attention should be given to the organization of the recording, its main points of emphasis, its unusual vocabulary, and questions which might grow out of its use.

*Develop appropriate class readiness for listening.* This may be done, in part, by providing an overview of the recording contents and by pointing out how it

[11]For a catalog of its current offerings, write to the Association for Educational Communications and Technology, 1201 Sixteenth Street, N.W., Washington, D.C. 20036.

relates to the work under way in the class. Explain the meanings of key items of vocabulary not likely to be already familiar. Indicate specific points to which the group should give particular attention while listening.

*Listen without interruption.* The mood of listening should be established, as appropriate. With some recordings, it may be desirable to dim room lights. The appropriateness of note-taking should also be considered. With some lengthy recordings, one or more breaks (with brief discussion) may be desirable.

*Hold a discussion or engage in other follow-up activities.* This will go back to the main points set up by the instructor during the prelistening introduction. It may be appropriate to repeat certain portions of the recording for emphasis. Check-tests are sometimes appropriate means of evaluating comprehension of the materials to which the class has listened.

## INSTRUCTOR- OR STUDENT-MADE RECORDINGS

Tape recording is widely practiced by both instructors and students in today's colleges and universities. Tape recording may make a number of distinctive contributions to one's teaching through: (a) interviews (by instructors or students), (b) absentee lectures or oral directions for the class to be used on occasional days when the instructor must be absent and prefers not to have a replacement, (c) recordings of meetings or conferences for later analysis or preparation as verbatim or outlined minutes or typescripts, (d) repeats of lectures for later auditioning by students who were absent or who wish to study them again, (e) standardized directions to be given identically to several different groups (as in the case of multiple test administrations), (f) "before and after" recordings (as, for example, those made during the first and last class sessions in a particular course), (g) audio records of field trips—including documentary sounds, oral "notes," interview records, and the like, (h) materials for exchange with professional acquaintances in other parts of the country or world, (i) recordings of valuable radio or TV (sound only) programs for personal reuse at convenient times, (j) recordings of the sound tracks of films shown in class—for later study and analysis after the films have been returned, or (k) edited excerpts from a number of different recordings put together in a new sequence for some special teaching or evaluation purpose.

It is a characteristic of tape recordings that they are easy to alter. They may be shortened, for example, to remove unwanted materials (some of which may be irrelevant or in need of editing or polishing); they may also be edited to reduce playing time to fit requirements of a rigid schedule; sequence of events may be rearranged to fit some special teaching situation, such as one requiring juxtaposing comments to provide contrast; they may be played back more slowly than they were recorded to permit unusual studies of sound details (as with the analysis of bird-song characteristics, for example).

As one of their services, most college audiovisual or learning resource centers will record radio programs, TV sound, speeches, musical performances, or similar audio events on request. There are many occasions, however, when instructors will prefer to prepare or edit their own. In that case, the following suggestions may prove helpful in improving quality:

Work from a prepared script or outline, if feasible. Interviews will be improved by writing out key questions in advance.

Reduce tape length to the minimum required by playing the original on one machine while stopping and starting a second to capture wanted portions of the original. In such cases, use two electrically connected recorders rather than picking up sound from the first through the microphone of the second.

Place microphone(s) and regulate gain (recording volume) carefully. The lower the gain is set, the less will be the pickup of extraneous background and crowd noises. Relatively low gain can be used without reducing the recording level by placing the microphone six to twelve inches from the speaker's mouth. Watch the recording volume indicator and adjust gain to avoid overmodulation and distortion.

It is not uncommon, of course, for the individual faculty member to own a tape recorder. Small, compact, transistorized, battery-operated tape recorders are becoming particularly popular as personal recorders because they free instructors to record almost anywhere at any time without need for access to power outlets.

### DUPLICATED AND OTHER PRINTED MATERIALS

College instructors use various forms of duplicated materials for teaching purposes. Duplicated materials are particularly useful as means of saving time when it is desired to communicate detailed information in uniform fashion to large classes.

Several different but fairly common forms of duplicating are available: spirit

**Figure 5-8.**
Modern photocopying devices of many different types have expanded the student's access
to various forms of data.

duplicating, mimeograph, offset and letterpress printing, and various forms of
photocopying. Personnel of the college or university press, the audiovisual or
learning resources center, or the library will usually be able to provide additional
information about each process. Essential details are as follows:

*The spirit duplicating* process uses aniline dye carbon papers (available in several
colors other than the traditional purple) to produce masters capable of
reproducing up to five hundred copies. This medium is particularly suited to
the usual requirements of college and university instructors. Producing the
master is a simple matter, and once it is made, the work can be run off
without delay. One possible disadvantage of the process, however, is that
copies do not last indefinitely; they tend to fade with time. Several colors can
be added to one master by using different colored carbons; the resulting
master then can produce finished work in a single run.

*The mimeograph process,* using a wax-coated stencil, permits preparation of
masters capable of reproducing several thousand copies, depending upon the

care with which they are handled. Copies are legible and will not fade; the last copy is as bright as the first. Different colored inks may be used to produce copy in different colors, but each color requires a separate run through the machine (and a cleanup between).

*Offset printing* (or photo-offset lithography) is a process which employs a sensitized metal plate to retain images of photographs or drawings or, sometimes, of a flexible cardboard plate which retains typing or drawing done with specially prepared typewriter carbons or ribbons or wax pencils. The medium is particularly valuable and economical for reproducing detailed drawings or halftones.

*Letterpress printing* is a process which prints from type, rather than metal or cardboard plates. When drawings or photographs are used with this process, etched halftones must be prepared. Because of the expense, it is not suited to the short runs required for classroom purposes.

*Photocopying*, as used here, refers generally to reproduction processes which provide in no more than a few seconds a paper duplicate of the original in "positive" form, i.e., the black lines of the original will reproduce as black lines, not white, in the copy.

Photocopying techniques such as Xerox are used in reproducing entire pages of books, rare manuscripts, drawings, and other items of special interest to the college instructor doing documentary research. It may also be useful as a means of providing a few additional copies of particularly valuable instructional materials to be placed on reserve.

College instructors must often make decisions about the propriety of reproducing materials for use in their classes. Claims pertaining to copyright infringements are not unknown, although the number made public appears to be small. Actually, the privilege of reproducing and distributing published materials belongs exclusively to the copyright holder, as shown at the front of copyrighted works, and any substantial appropriation of the works of an original author, without his specific permission, constitutes copyright piracy.

Instructors are cautioned, therefore, to be particularly careful to secure advance permission to reprint copyrighted materials (even in hectographed or mimeographed form) whether or not footnoted acknowledgments of sources are made and whether or not they are sold or given gratis to students. Similar cautions apply to the copying of photographs and drawings.

## SUMMARY

Chapter Five discusses the rationale and procedures for utilization of instructional resources in higher education. The rationale may be summarized in seven points: (1) teaching resources are adopted to facilitate, not to dictate, teaching objectives; (2) because courses and instructors differ, it is more often necessary to develop individually produced resources rather than to purchase them; (3) no single medium is universally effective; (4) time and effort are required to develop resources, but the resulting improvement in learning often justifies the effort; (5) there are many acceptable ways of using instructional resources; (6) resources do not replace instructors—they supplement and enlarge their effectiveness; and (7) no instructor should expect to use all of the resources described.

The remainder of the chapter presents descriptions of resources, and practical suggestions for use, together with source references. The entire chapter is designed to assist instructors to plan systematically and to choose a battery of nonhuman resources that will enliven and improve their teaching effectiveness.

## RELATED READING

Briggs, Leslie J., et al. *Instructional Media.* Pittsburgh: American Institutes for Research, 1967.

Brown, James W., Richard B. Lewis, and Fred F. Harcleroad. *AV Instruction: Media and Methods.* New York: McGraw-Hill Book Company, 1969.

Dale, Edgar. *Audiovisual Methods in Teaching.* New York: Holt, Rinehart and Winston, Inc., 1969.

Harcleroad, Fred F. (principal investigator). *Learning Resources for Colleges and Universities.* Hayward, California: California State College at Hayward, 1964.

Johnson, B. Lamar (ed.). *The Junior College Library.* Los Angeles: University of California, 1966.

Loughary, John W. *Man-Machine Systems in Education.* New York: Harper and Row, 1966.

Stewart, David C. (ed.). *Film Study in Higher Education.* Washington: American Council on Education, 1966.

Torkelson, Gerald M. *Educational Media.* Washington: National Education Association, 1968.

Weisberger, Robert A. (ed.). *Instructional Process and Media Innovation.* Chicago: Rand McNally and Company, 1968.

Wiman, Raymond V., and Wesley C. Meierhenry. *Educational Media: Theory into Practice.* Columbus, Ohio: Charles E. Merrill Publishing Company, 1969.

# chapter six / EVALUATING INSTRUCTION / STEPS IN EVALUA-
TION • TESTS IN EVALUATION • POSSIBLE EFFECTS OF
TESTS • ADMINISTERING TESTS • ESSAY TESTS • OBJEC-
TIVE TESTS • IMPROVING OBJECTIVE TESTS • JUDGING
OTHER STUDENT WORK • GRADING • MEASURING INTER-
ESTS AND ATTITUDES • EVALUATING THE INSTRUCTOR •
EVALUATING LECTURING TECHNIQUES • SUMMARY • RE-
LATED READING

An essential step in any systematic plan for college teaching involves the feedback and evaluation of outcomes. The college instructor's complete program of evaluation, which should really be regarded as an important continuous aspect of teaching, allows him to accomplish several purposes, as follows:

To determine, through feedback, the level of knowledge, other achievement, or condition of students in his classes at various times during the term

To provide bases for assigning grades

To become aware of specific difficulties of individual students, or of the entire class, as a basis for further teaching

To estimate the effectiveness of techniques, subject content, and instructional resources in reaching the goals of his course

To encourage students' learning by measuring their achievement, by informing them of their success, and by reinforcing the emphasis of class presentations through repetitions on tests

To use the additional motivation of examinations to provide practice in critical thinking

To gather information needed for administrative purposes, such as selecting students for honors courses, permitting students to enter sequential courses, granting credit by examination, meeting graduation requirements, writing recommendations, or assessing facets of institutional quality

To serve as a basis for replanning and improving the next offering of the course.

Chapter Six deals with concepts of evaluation related to all these purposes. It discusses the development and improvement of several varieties of classroom tests; it presents suggestions for uses of other measures of achievement, including some of the less obvious and concrete outcomes of instruction, such as attitudes and interests and skills of abstraction; and it gives some attention to the instructor's own evaluation of his effectiveness as a teacher. Because some of the kinds of data require mathematical treatment, elementary statistical concepts and operations are introduced quite briefly.

## STEPS IN EVALUATION

The total process of evaluating instruction may be arranged in a series of sequential steps, even though in actual operation the experienced instructor may accomplish several steps at one time or perhaps assume that he has completed one or another before and that he need not recognize it explicitly again. However, the new instructor will do well to use the following points as a checklist of the adequacy of his course evaluation:

*Develop a clear statement of instructional objectives.* Obviously, progress cannot be perceived and assessed unless base points have been determined and intended direction made clear. Considerations involved in developing course objectives related to these requirements were discussed in Chapter Three; they are worth repeating.

*List and briefly describe situations in which students can demonstrate their degree of achievement of these objectives.* If the development of the ability to think critically is an objective, what kinds of problem situations will allow students to demonstrate that they can do it? What kinds of evidence will aid in judging the level of student knowledge of facts, understanding of principles or generalizations, interests or attitudes, or proficiency in skills related to the course?

*Develop systematic means of eliciting kinds of behavior implied in objectives to be evaluated.* To obtain reliable measures of such behavior, sampling must usually occur in not one but several different situations. To permit comparisons of individuals and to remove, insofar as possible, effects of inconsistencies in problem presentations or of instructor bias, tests or other instruments should be administered in a standardized manner.

*Develop means of recording information about students in these problem situations.* Such means may involve written tests, performance tests, attitude scales, rating scales, project assignments (papers, reports, creative constructions, experiments), case analyses, or others.

*Develop means of quantifying objectively the information received in the situations described above.* This may involve assigning weight factors to adjust scores for variability or the relative importance of the learning products evaluated. It may also involve decisions about criteria for scoring: number of correct responses, quality of reasoning revealed through responses, or manner of expressing responses.

*Establish conditions which permit the student to give his best performance.* Distracting conversation during a student report, or constant hammering outside the window during an essay test, may contaminate the measurement. So also might cheating, confusing test directions, or unfair questions.

*Assign scores on the basis of the above steps.* Check to determine that there is sufficient variance in them to permit achievement of the purposes of the evaluation.

*Check the validity, reliability, and difficulty of measures used.* For classroom tests, such checks are usually rather simple, but the instructor should perform them periodically and strive to improve his measuring instruments and his own use of them.

*Consider implications of all data in evaluating student progress and performance and the effectiveness of the course as a whole.* Look for ways of providing needed changes or refinements to produce better results the next time the course is taught.


## TESTS IN EVALUATION


Probably the most common means of obtaining data with which to evaluate changes in one's students is the written test. A test has been defined as an instrument which permits "sinking shafts at critical points"; here we use the term operationally to describe a systematic series of questions or tasks designed to sample and measure knowledge, skills, performance, or similar behavior of students. Its chief purpose is to yield scores so that the level of achievement of the different students may be compared. Various types of rating scales (recording data concerning attitudes, interest, creative constructions, or other forms of class participation) are discussed separately, although their classification as tests would be consistent with the above definition. In both cases, discussion is limited to *instructor-made* instruments for use in the classroom.

Different instructional objectives must be evaluated by different types of instructor-made tests; but similar criteria can be applied in judging them. Instructors will usually seek tests that (1) provide an adequate sample of the objectives of the course, and (2) adequately sample the content of the course. They must also be (3) valid, (4) reliable, (5) practical, and (6) useful. Each of these criteria will be discussed briefly, in turn.

## SAMPLING COURSE OBJECTIVES

Although Chapter Three emphasized the variety of objectives for courses in the college curriculum, it should come as no surprise that the objective, "knowledge of essential facts," frequently receives more than its share of attention in instructor-made tests. Probably this is because questions relating to this objective are easier to construct than items measuring abilities to use those facts in solving problems, making judgments, or in drawing conclusions. The undebatable nature of factual questions, as compared with thought questions, tends to encourage their use. But measures of other important objectives must not be neglected, despite the fact that considerable skill and ingenuity are sometimes needed to develop practical tests for them.

## SAMPLING COURSE CONTENT

The factual content of the usual college course includes literally thousands of related items, some more important than others. The instructor has no choice but to select from among all possible items a relative few to include in his tests. When he does, he assumes that student performance on this smaller sample will be similar to the performance a student might have made on a longer test containing all possible content items. In choosing the sample, therefore, he must be certain there are *enough* items and that they are *representative* of the range of course content. Samples containing unbalanced emphases may produce inaccurately weighted results. Instructors sometimes check the adequacy of their sample of content by preparing a tabulation of questions relating to each important topic of the course.

### TEST VALIDITY

A test, to be valid, must measure what it is supposed or is said to measure—not unintentionally something else. A test may have high validity for use in one situation, but low validity for another (as, for example, an economics test designed for college freshmen but used instead with seniors, or one designed to measure mathematical skills which, because of its complex language, measures reading ability instead). If the instructor's test contains unbalanced emphases on some course objectives or some aspects of course content, or if it includes items unrelated to what has been taught or assigned, its validity as a measure of achievement in the *total course* is reduced. A valid test will allow a student to demonstrate the degree to which he has the ability or quality measured, without such inappropriate influences upon his performance. Aspects of assessing and improving test validity are discussed later in this chapter.

### TEST RELIABILITY

A reliable test measures consistently and accurately—each time it is used. Its results are not unduly influenced by chance. A reliable test provides nearly the same score for a student each time he takes it, unless his ability has been changed by study, maturation, disease, or other influence. The similarity in successive scores is a measure of a test's reliability. In the same way, a test is reliable to the extent that a reliable or competent scorer on different readings, or two different reliable or competent scorers, assign similar scores to the same paper. Techniques and procedures involved in estimating and improving test reliability are discussed later in this chapter.

### TEST PRACTICALITY

Practical tests are capable of being administered and scored with reasonable ease and within the limitations of time or resources imposed by the circumstances of their use. Individual performance tests often have exceptionally high validity as measures of true ability, but the time required to administer them—one student at a time—and to score and interpret the results may be out of all proportion to their utility. Typically, the instructor must choose other more practical means of measuring the achievements with which he is concerned— most often through paper-and-pencil tests which sample ability through indirect means.

### TEST USEFULNESS

Two common uses of tests by college instructors are to provide bases for assigning fair grades and to obtain evidence about their own teaching effectiveness. But there are also other uses for them. If the instructor wishes to determine how well each student has mastered certain fundamentals (for example, by means of a pretest at the beginning of a course), he may design and use a *mastery* test which contains items measuring essential and basic content. Analysis of results would indicate course areas likely to require extra attention during the term or the necessary amount of review which must be undertaken before proceeding with more advanced material.

If, on the other hand, the instructor wishes to measure the *speed* with which his students are capable of working (i.e., how far they are capable of going in a test within a specified period of time), items will need to be sufficiently easy to permit almost every student to answer them correctly if they were given enough time to do so.

Usually what is wanted, however, is a *power* test which gives each student time and opportunity to work to a level very close to his capacity. Most students will be expected to finish such tests, but those who do not will have done, by definition, as much as they are capable of doing. The range and distribution of scores resulting from such tests provide suitable bases for assigning rank-order performance ratings or grades and give information about teaching effectiveness as well.

### POSSIBLE EFFECTS OF TESTS

General consideration of the role of tests in evaluating achievement of college students must not overlook their potentially deleterious effects. It is widely known, for example, that the types of tests students expect to be given influence their manner of preparing for them. If students know they will be expected to recall large numbers of isolated facts, for example, rather than to apply ideas or principles derived from reading and other class experiences, they will give more attention to such details in preparing for examinations. Concerning this, Bloom comments:

> Much more research is needed on this vital aspect of the learning process. What occurs when the learning experiences and the examinations emphasize contradictory objectives? . . . It does seem clear that if the major reward-penalty system is related to examination performance, the students will concentrate on preparation for the examinations by any means at their disposal. . . . (The) question may be asked: "How can examinations be used to encourage particular types of learning by the students?" If it is desired that students do a great deal of independent study and thinking, how should the examinations be constructed and used to promote such study and thinking? If it is desired that students develop a high degree of creativity in their thinking, research, and writing, how can examinations be developed and used to promote this? Perhaps as we understand how examinations may be used to promote rigid thinking and rote memorization, we will be in a better position to know how to use examinations to prevent this and to develop the characteristics explicitly desired by the objectives of instruction.[1]

## ADMINISTERING TESTS

Environmental conditions surrounding the administration of tests are known to influence the quality of student performance on them. The student who is emotionally disturbed, physically exhausted, unmotivated to succeed with test tasks, confused by directions, or successful in cheating on a test will not demonstrate his true ability with respect to it—thereby invalidating the results of his performance.

Physical conditions of test administration must therefore be attended to: comfortable temperature, adequate ventilation, a seating arrangement which discourages cheating, suitable lighting, and freedom from distracting noise or

[1] Benjamin S. Bloom, "Testing Cognitive Ability and Achievement," in *Handbook of Research on Teaching*, ed. Nathaniel Gage (Chicago: Rand McNally and Company, 1963), pp. 392-393.

interruption. Motivation toward maximum effort on the test usually requires little more than a clarification by the instructor of the uses to be made of results.

Test directions must also be clear to avoid invalidating confusions and inaccurate completion of test tasks by students who really possess the ability measured. Clarity may be improved by following the practice of spending a few moments at the beginning of the period to go over the test, correcting typographical errors, indicating suggested time limits, answering questions, and reminding the class of procedures and weights to be used in scoring its various parts.

Cheating, as an aspect of test administration, presents special problems of concern to the instructor. But its incidence may be reduced by careful attention to a few details, as suggested by the following:

Protect test security by regularly revising tests and by using special care in typing, duplicating, assembling, and storing test materials. Students testify that most cheating occurs through advance knowledge of test content, caused largely by instructor inattention to these details.

Number all test booklets, and ask that they be returned with bluebooks or answer sheets.

Spread out chairs, if possible, or ask students to occupy every other seat.

Monitor the room as the test proceeds, unless other arrangements are required. If cheating is suspected, note students' names to identify papers for later analysis. In most cases, cheating within the test room may be discouraged by careful attention in advance to competent test administration.

Give different forms of the same test to different sections of the same class, or give them in succeeding terms.

Alternate test forms may be developed quite simply by duplicating tests in sections of twenty to thirty items each. These sections are then arranged in two (or more) different orders, suitably identified by the instructor, and distributed to students who occupy adjoining seats. Another convenient way to develop alternate test forms is to distribute the same pages of test items in two or more arrangement combinations without prior numbering of items. Students are then asked to number their own items consecutively. Again, scoring arrangements must be changed for each different form of arrangement of the pages.

## ESSAY TESTS

Essay tests are highly regarded by most college instructors for whose courses they are appropriate and by some for whom they are not. They are believed by many professors to be capable of measuring the "higher mental processes"— summarizing; presenting arguments for or against; evaluating rationality and suitability of conclusions, or proposed or actual courses of action, writing creatively; and similar intellectual tasks.

However, experienced instructors are also aware of the disadvantages of essay tests. While they are relatively easy to prepare, they require considerably more time than objective tests to read and score. Since the student presents responses in his own words, with his own style, organization, and spelling, they are often unstructured and unstandardized. It is difficult to judge correctness or quality with any reliable degree of objectivity. Sampling of student knowledge can be deep and detailed in areas covered by questions; but both the limited number of questions which can be asked in essay tests and the difficulty of achieving objectivity in scoring reduce the reliability of results. The essay test may require the student to recall, interpret, or analyze rather than to identify a correct, ready-prepared alternative response as in a multiple-choice item. The instructor, therefore, frequently experiences difficulty in separating poor spelling, poor handwriting, or poor style or organization from the student's real ability with respect to the subject of the question.

### DEVELOPING SATISFACTORY ESSAY QUESTIONS

The special difficulties which instructors encounter with essay questions suggest three procedures which will improve their quality and usefulness, as follows:

*Essay questions should capitalize upon their unique advantages.* Questions are recommended which require students to "tell why," "criticize," "contrast," "summarize," "compare," "explain why," "trace the development of," "give examples," or "evaluate." Questions asking students to name individuals, give dates, assign titles, define terms, make lists, or enumerate usually may be presented more effectively in objective form.

*Essay questions should be stated unambiguously.* Good essay test items should convey to the student the meanings intended by the instructor who wrote them. Ambiguity can be reduced by economical use of language, by careful attention to the framing of questions, by thinking of likely responses of students to the wording employed, by trying out questions with one's colleagues or students before they are used in class, and by revising items, after use, which experience shows are faulty.

*Essay questions should call for structured responses of somewhat limited scope.* A common fault of essay questions is that they are too broad in scope. Obviously, the broader the range of acceptable response to essay questions, the more difficult it is to compare one student's response with another and the less reliable its scoring is likely to be. One means of ameliorating (if not eliminating) this problem is to indicate in the question itself the scope of the expected answer. This may be aided by avoiding use of vague words such as "describe," "discuss," or "tell about," without further restrictive words or phrases.

The so-called open-book essay examination lends itself to evaluation of the student's ability to find, assess, and use information rather than simply to recall or restate it. To many, it represents a superior means of determining the degree to which a student knows sources of information and how to use them rather than simply to recall facts which may or may not be appropriate to the purpose. Good questions for the open-book essay test require the student to integrate, interpret, synthesize, or generalize—not to quote verbatim responses from books he consults. The open-book examination is sometimes given in the library itself, with a set time period allotted for completion of assignments and full freedom to use all resources in the building.

### IMPROVING RELIABILITY OF ESSAY TESTS

A common criticism of essay tests is that they are unreliable. Their reliability may be improved, however, by delimiting and structuring the items as discussed above and by carrying out procedures such as the following:

Determine, first, whether an absolute or relative scale of scoring will be used. When operating from the absolute frame of reference, the instructor determines arbitrarily the standards to be used in assigning a certain grade or score without regard to a curve of performance for the class as a whole. If the relative scale is used, however, the following procedures will apply.

Read the same question in all papers, *seriatim*, rather than one complete paper at
a time. This procedure, and that of concealing student names, helps to reduce
the halo effect (the carry-over of judgment from one question to another on
the same paper, or from other knowledge about the student, to his performance on the test as a whole). Too, it provides better bases for making
comparisons of answers.

Apply predetermined criteria for judging the quality of student responses. An
itemized checklist may be used as a reminder of facts, principles, generalizations, conclusions, evidence, or sources of authority. Instructors sometimes
make check marks on papers to indicate the presence of expected elements
and then use the total of such marks as the basis for a grade on the question.

For each answer read, sort papers into several piles (from five to nine are
recommended). Make the judgment that "this paper is better than that one,
poorer than this one." Move papers into different piles as further comparisons
are made.

It is generally agreed that the practice of permitting students the option of
selecting essay questions they will answer in the test (such as "Answer three of
the following five questions.") reduces the value of comparisons of student
performance on the test as a whole, since the students, in effect, are taking
different tests.

## OBJECTIVE TESTS

College instructors desiring to use test types appropriate to the outcomes they
seek will usually employ objective as well as essay items. Rapid development of
objective tests was stimulated in part by the studies of Starch and Elliott[2] who
found exceptionally low agreement on ratings of nonobjective papers in high
school English and mathematics classes when scored by different instructors.
The improved reliability and validity of properly constructed objective tests, as
compared with essay tests (fairly well established by the early thirties), led to
their increased use at all levels and to the development of many variations of the

---

[2]D. Starch and E. C. Elliott, "Reliability of Grading High School Work in English," *School
Review,* 20 (1912): 442-457. "Reliability of Grading Work in History," *School Review,*
21 (1913): 676-681. "Reliability of Grading High School Work in Mathematics," *School
Review,* 21 (1913): 254-259.

basic factual answer item. Useful varieties of items include the true-false, multiple-choice, matching, completion and short-answer, and identification. After certain general suggestions are presented, each of these will be discussed.

### ADVANTAGES AND DISADVANTAGES OF OBJECTIVE TESTS

Objective tests have several advantages to recommend their use in college teaching. First, because they are brief and require only a minimum of writing by the student, a considerable number of objective items may be included in a single test. Course content and course objectives may thus be sampled widely. This, in turn, improves the fairness of the test to a student who may be completely blank on a single narrow aspect of the work. Another advantage of objective tests is that they can be made quite reliable. With modest effort, items can be written so as to reduce inconsistencies of scoring by persons having different opinions about "correct" answers or other qualities of responses. A third advantage of objective tests which appeals to instructors of large classes is that they permit accurate scoring, with a key, by clerical personnel or machines. The time required for this task is usually less than for essay tests.

Several apparent disadvantages of objective tests should also be mentioned. One is that a good objective test requires a considerable amount of time to prepare. But the time saved through simplified scoring procedures and the opportunity to reuse good items in future tests aid in counteracting this disadvantage. Two other alleged disadvantages are still being debated: that objective tests encourage poor study habits through emphasizing unimportant details and that, because answers are usually checked rather than formulated in the student's own words, they hamper the improvement of writing ability.

### SUGGESTIONS FOR PREPARING OBJECTIVE TESTS

The criteria for satisfactory tests developed earlier in this chapter also apply generally to the development of objective tests; additional specific suggestions will aid in their preparation:

Prepare tests of sufficient length to provide reliable results. As a check against omitting items measuring important objectives or content, prepare a two-dimensional grid. Put course topics in a list down the left-hand side; arrange course objectives in columns across the top. Check and insert item numbers in appropriate columns as they are completed. Note and correct gaps which develop.

Choose a variety of test items for the special contributions each can make to the measurements sought.

Seek to measure one important thing with each separately scored item. Avoid using the answer to one question as a key part of a following item.

Write items in a straightforward manner, avoiding tricky phrasing, double negatives, unfamiliar words, ambiguities, or unnecessary verbiage. Be as brief as possible without sacrificing meaning. A test should be a measure, not a puzzle. Avoid quoting from the text.

Avoid too many easy items (except for mastery or speed tests) which can be answered correctly by everyone in the class.

Randomize correct responses so that students do not detect some system which may have been employed to facilitate scoring.

Ask a colleague to read items to check clarity and to see how a person familiar with the material responds to them. Revise and simplify wording or format, as suggested.

Assemble items of one type in the same test section; do not intermix. Precede each section with a part number and a set of directions. If necessary, include sample questions to guide response patterns.

## TRUE-FALSE ITEMS

True-false test items, usually consisting of single statements to be marked "true" or "false," have been criticized for several important reasons. Since there is a fifty-fifty chance of one's being able to answer such questions correctly whether or not he knows anything about them, the form encourages guessing. Too, undeniably true or false items are difficult to construct; there are so many qualifications to influence answers. Finally, the true-false format tempts some instructors to prepare items through the simple process of altering textbook statements, thus encouraging in students the wrong kinds of learning and the wrong kinds of preparation for tests.

But true-false items do have the special advantage of permitting the instructor to sample widely from among course elements. They are also sufficiently brief to permit economical duplication in test-sheet form, and they are easily scored. If constructed with care they have certain limited contributions to make in measuring achievement in college classes, especially ability to recall essential facts.

Following are several general suggestions for developing true-false tests:

Use at least forty to fifty items in a quiz and one hundred items in a regular examination; shorter tests reduce reliability.

A combination of two or more types of questions is preferable to a test composed solely of true-false items.

Divide true and false items in about equal proportions and distribute in random fashion throughout the test.

Avoid using such words as "all," "only," "most," "frequently," "never," "generally," "always."

Simplify statements as much as possible; avoid double negatives or unnecessarily involved sentences.

Avoid trivia; develop items which require students to think with what they have learned rather than simply to recall it.

Avoid making true items consistently longer or shorter than false items.

Several variations of simple true-false items are sometimes used. With one type, the item may be written so that all but the stem is underlined. The student is asked to react to the complete statement as it stands; if he considers it false, he must rewrite the underlined portion so as to make it true. Another type checks thinking ability by first presenting a statement which students rate as true or false and then asking them to check related statements which support their choice. Sometimes a main stem statement is given and followed by several statements to complete it. Students are asked to rate each completion statement as true or false. Another variation is to ask students to check items as "true," "probably true," "probably false," or "false."

### MULTIPLE-CHOICE ITEMS

A multiple-choice item usually consists of a statement or question accompanied by several choices or answers—of which only one is correct, or "best." The multiple-choice form has several advantages over the true-false form just discussed. It is generally regarded as a useful means of measuring certain higher level mental functions (critical thinking, comparison, judgment) which are difficult or impossible to measure with true-false questions; it lowers chances of success through mere guessing; and it permits the presentation of test situations in the more lifelike circumstances of "choices to be made."

Following are several general suggestions for developing improved multiple-choice items:

Generally speaking, provide with each item only one correct or best answer. (See additional comments below concerning a variation of this procedure.)

Write four or five alternative responses for each item; try to make each response plausible.

Test one main (and important) idea or course aspect with each item.

Relate ideas for the stem and responses within items; avoid a spread of ideas within the same item.

Pack as much of the item as possible into the stem; make responses brief and clear and of approximately equal length.

Make sure that statements proceed grammatically from the end of the stem to the end of each response.

Strive for clear expression; avoid confusion caused by unnecessary length, ambiguity, or tricky or abstruse language.

Underline words like *not* or *all except* to avoid their being overlooked.

Avoid making correct responses brief and clear and incorrect ones long and involved.

Do not reveal answers by the use of "a" or "an" at the end of the stem.

Scatter correct responses in random order.

Avoid questions which can be answered on the basis of general knowledge rather than on what has been learned in the course.

Use novel data in items which require thinking and application of principles rather than recall of information exclusively; avoid items which are verbatim from the text.

List response choices in columns, rather than in paragraph form; for ease of scoring, provide a uniformly placed space with each item in which to record answers (or use a standard answer sheet).

Several variations of the above procedures may be used to provide functional measurements of some instructional outcomes which cannot be presented adequately in problem form through usual verbal means:

Use visual materials as part of the standardized presentation of item stems or response choices. For example, prepare a large transparency containing several pictures or drawings, of which one is the best answer to a problem. Several smaller 2- by 2-inch slides may also be laid on the projection surface to provide materials for the items.

Base several written questions on a projected still picture or a portion of an unfamiliar motion picture (perhaps one projected silently, with sound turned off).

As part of the problem material for a test, give a demonstration accompanied by a carefully prepared oral commentary explaining or commenting upon tasks performed. Prepare written questions which measure the ability of students to judge the accuracy, correctness of order, or validity of explanations accompanying the demonstration.

Use prepared tape or disk recordings of quoted or dramatized materials on which to base questions. Specially selected (original or quoted) written statements may also be used similarly.

Include reproductions of drawings, graphs, or photographs in items within tests given to students.

## MATCHING ITEMS

Matching items are generally composed of two related lists of words, phrases, symbols, or pictures. The test task is to match each item in the first list with the most closely related or appropriate item in the second. Matching items are particularly helpful in measuring the ability of students to relate principles to situations in which those principles operate, to select correct definitions of terms, or to tie causes to effects.

Following are several general suggestions for the improved preparation of matching items:

Make the alternative answer list longer than the problem list (unless directions specifically indicate that each alternative may be used more than once).

Make problems and responses in each matching question deal with one subject.

Use at least five but no more than twelve problems in each item.

Make items brief without sacrificing meaning.

Avoid splitting matching items on parts of two pages.

Arrange possible problems and answers in some readily discernible manner (alphabetically, chronologically, logically).

## COMPLETION AND SHORT-ANSWER ITEMS

Completion and short-answer questions require the respondent to fill in blanks with one or more words or phrases which he himself has recalled or developed to complete the thought or to answer the question. The blanks themselves may be within emasculated sentences (_____ followed Churchill as British Prime Minister after the fall of Germany in World War II.); or they may be single words, phrases, or numbers in answers to direct questions (What is the latest estimate of the population of the United States?_____).

Completion and short-answer questions cannot be scored so objectively as some other types of questions discussed in this section. Consequently, their scoring usually cannot be handled by one unfamiliar with the nature of various acceptable answers. However, both types of questions are particularly useful in measuring ability to recall specifics, such as names of individuals, dates of events, place names, titles or authors of books, ability to solve mathematical problems (leaving space for inserting correct answers), and for similar purposes.

Suggestions for improving completion and short-answer questions follow:

Avoid indefinite completion items which can be answered correctly in several different ways. Structure each item so that the correct answer is clear to the person who really knows it.

Avoid giveaway articles (a, an), as well as singular and plural antecedents, which may provide clues to answers.

Restrict blanks to key words and do not omit so many that sentences resemble puzzles. Do not omit sentence verbs (as in "Marat_____the _____ of_____ in _____.").

For ease of scoring, require answers to be written or marked uniformly along the margin of the test page or on a separate answer sheet.

## SCORING OBJECTIVE TESTS

The scoring of objective tests may be carried out in several ways. When only a few papers are involved, hand scoring is recommended and such scoring will be facilitated by requiring students to use standard answer sheets. A scoring stencil can be made by punching holes over the correct answers. As this stencil is then placed over each answer sheet, correct answers may be spotted. Holes in which no markings appear will be scored wrong; items must be checked for double markings which are to be considered wrong also.

Another type of hand-scoring stencil may be made from strips of stiff paper on which are typed or pasted the properly spaced numbers for test items, with correct answers indicated. Scoring is simplified by placing this key strip alongside the numbered columns on the answer sheet.

Machine scoring of objective tests (usually recommended for fifty or more papers) is a boon to college teaching. Automatic scorers are capable of providing several types of readings: (1) number of right answers, (2) number of wrong answers, (3) number of rights minus number of wrongs, (4) number of rights plus number of wrongs, (5) subtotals of such figures for different test sections, and (6) tabulations of the number of responses to individual choices for multiple-choice items.

### CORRECTING FOR GUESSING

When students have a reasonable chance of reading and responding to all items in an objective test within the time allotted (as is nearly always the case with instructor-made power tests), corrections for chance are usually considered unnecessary.

It should be remembered, of course, that one might expect half the items in a true-false test to be answered correctly on a purely chance basis, while on a four-response multiple-choice test a fourth of them could be. The *effective* range of a 100-item true-false test, then, would really be between 50 and 100; for a 100-item, four-choice multiple-choice test, between 25 and 100. This means, essentially, that the student who scores 70 in a 100-item true-false test might "know" (as measured by the test) only 20 points better than chance rather than 70 percent of the area measured by the test. "True" scores of performances in other test types are also reduced accordingly.

### IMPROVING OBJECTIVE TESTS

It is important, of course, to continually improve one's objective tests and to revise them as necessary for use with future classes. Improvement involves a search for answers to several questions:

How well does each item in the test discriminate among persons of different levels of ability in areas measured by the test as a whole? (Item discrimination) How difficult is the test as a whole? (Test difficulty) How difficult are

individual items? Too easy? Too difficult? About right? (Item difficulty) Is
the test about the right length? Are items stated clearly and unambiguously?
Are the items fair? Is the test reliable? Does the test yield a sufficiently broad
range of scores on which to base a satisfactory grading pattern?

The feedback expected of these analyses is indicated by still another question: Does the test suggest learning or teaching difficulties and clues for dealing
with them?

Answers to many of these questions may be determined through three
processes: (1) studying the total *scores* and the *distribution of responses* students make to each item on the test, (2) determining statistically the *discrimination power* of each item on the test, and (3) determining the *difficulty* of each
item.

### STUDYING SCORES AND DISTRIBUTION OF ITEM RESPONSES

A study of scores on tests and of responses to test items may be carried out as
follows:

Arrange all test papers, by order of score, from highest to lowest. Papers with
identical scores may be placed in random order at a point following the
preceding higher score.

Count papers from the bottom to include approximately one-third of the total
number of papers for the group taking the test; this is the low group. Count
an identical number of cases from the top; this is the high group.

Prepare a chart (see sample following) to tabulate responses to each alternative
choice for each test item, and make separate entries for high and low groups.
Mark the correct response for each item.[3]

| Item no. | Group | Responses | | | | | |
|----------|-------|-----------|-----|-----|-----|-----|-------------|
|          |       | Omitted   | A   | B   | C   | D   | Not reached |
| 1.       | High  | 5         | 23  | 50* | 10  | 12  |             |
|          | Low   | 8         | 35  | 10* | 42  | 3   | 2           |

*Correct answer

Examine tallies for all items to find any which are (1) missed by all students in
high and low groups, (2) missed by more students in the high than in the low

---

[3] A similar chart can be made for completion-type questions by substituting "right" and
"wrong" for "A-B-C-D" shown here.

group. All such items and distractors should be examined further to determine whether they are ambiguous or misleading or whether they actually have second correct answers. It appears that the sample item in the chart above made good discrimination between the high and low groups in the class (fifty versus ten correct answers). This suggests the item has satisfactory discrimination.

Examine tallies as well, to determine how distractors operated. In the sample above, distractors A and C drew large numbers of students who did not know the correct answer, but distractor D (which drew more responses from those in the high group than from the low) should be studied to determine whether it needs rewording or is also another correct response to the item.

Make a further examination to determine the frequency of "not reached" tallies, especially toward the end of the test. This analysis will permit some judgment as to whether the test was too long. It is usually desirable in course achievement tests to have at least 90 percent of the class try all questions.

### STUDYING ITEM DISCRIMINATION

If more persons who performed well in a test as a whole mark a single item correctly than do those who performed poorly in the test, that item is said to have positive discrimination—an assumed measure of validity. If the reverse is true, it has negative discrimination. Generally speaking, items of negative or low positive discrimination should be revised or eliminated, at least for future uses. Simple inspection of tabulated results of the performance of high and low groups (upper and lower thirds) is usually all that is needed to assess the quality of item discrimination. If additional accuracy is desired, however, one may use any of several methods of computation. One simple procedure produces a combined discrimination and difficulty index. It involves (1) finding the difference between high- and low-group students who answered items correctly, and (2) dividing that number by the maximum possible difference (defined as equaling the number of students in the upper group). In the case of the sample in the chart above, the difference was 40; the maximum possible difference was 100; and the ratio obtained by dividing 100 into 40 is .40. For most purposes achievement test items with negative or low (0 to .20) discrimination indices are considered poor (and thus need reworking); those from .20 to .40 are average; and those above .40 show superior discrimination.

## STUDYING ITEM AND TEST DIFFICULTY

Separate evidence of *test item* difficulty can be obtained from further study of the distribution of responses of the upper and lower groups in the example discussed above. An item difficulty index may be obtained, in such cases, simply by dividing the total number of responses (which for the sample item above is 200) into the total number of correct responses (which for this item is 60, giving an item difficulty index of .30).

If, as is usually the case, the purpose of a multiple-choice test is to discriminate among students of different achievement levels with respect to course objectives and content, it should contain items in the middle-to-difficult range. This means that one should aim to produce a total test for which the *average score* is approximately equal to fifty percent of the items (i.e., an average of 50 percent of all items, taken together, will be answered correctly and 50 percent will be answered incorrectly by the students). To achieve this balance for the total test, however, it is recommended that its individual items vary in difficulty from perhaps the 15 percent to the 85 percent levels.

It may be seen, of course, that with true-false tests a middle-to-difficult item would be more nearly one which could be answered correctly by 75 percent of the class, since, on a chance basis alone, it could be answered correctly 50 percent of the time.

Some data for evaluating the difficulty of the test as a whole may be obtained by studying the distribution of scores. If, in a test of 100 items, a top score of 52 is earned by only one student and there is a downward distribution of scores from that point to 12, it is obvious that the test is difficult. If, in another test of 100 items, the top score is 100 and the lowest 84, it is clear that the test is easy. When tests are quite difficult, scores tend to pile up at the low end of the distribution, producing what is known as positive skewness. When tests are too easy, negative skewness results. In the latter case, relative differences among student performances on the test are largely lost. The phenomenon of skewness, as contrasted with normal or symmetrical distributions, is plotted in Figure 6-1.

## DISCUSSING TESTS WITH STUDENTS

By discussing tests with students, one may uncover clues to reasons for wrong responses, and derive suggestions on how to improve items found to be functioning improperly. When such analyses turn up items with negative discrimination,

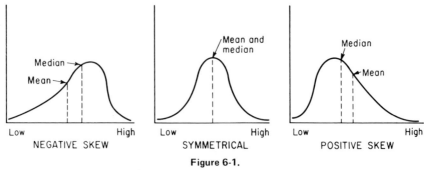

Figure 6-1.
Skewness in test score distributions.

discussion will usually indicate why individuals with greatest ability (as measured by performance on the test as a whole) were misled by the item content which less able students tended to ignore. Discussions also provide data regarding student opinion of the test's fairness and identify item ambiguities.

### STUDYING TEACHING AND LEARNING DIFFICULTIES

Analyses of test item responses also provide leads about difficulties of instruction or learning. Such analyses should be approached with several important questions in mind: Do the students as a group (the more capable ones in particular) answer questions dealing with some topics or objectives less accurately than others? Do item tallies suggest strengths or weaknesses of identifiable class presentations or activities (e.g., film showings, visiting lecturers, assigned reading, field trips)? What do students say, during later interviews, about these activities? Will reteaching or additional makeup assignments be required?

### STUDYING TEST RELIABILITY

Test reliability—a concept introduced earlier in this chapter—is a measure of the consistency or accuracy of test measurement, each time it is used. A reliable test is not influenced unduly by chance. Test reliability may be estimated in several ways, the simplest of which is through use of "scattergrams" based on scores derived from split halves of a test as a whole. With this procedure it is recommended that the instructor use two scoring keys and obtain one score for

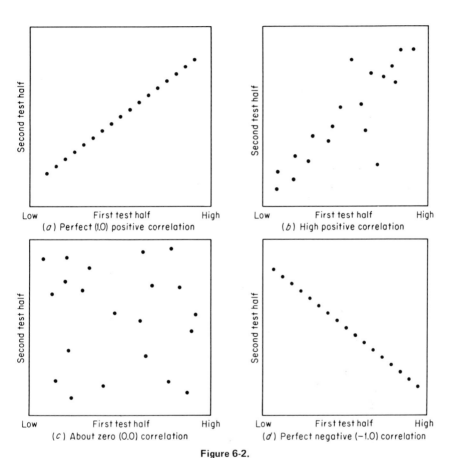

**Figure 6-2.**

Correlation of test halves. Source: Adapted from Dorothy Adkins Wood, *Test Construction: Development and Interpretation of Achievement Tests* (Columbus, Ohio: Charles E. Merrill Books, Inc., 1961), pp. 78-79.

odd and one for even items in the test.[4] Each set of scores is then plotted on a scattergram, as shown in Figure 6-2. The perfect positive linear relationship (as shown in Chart A) will never be achieved. But if it were to be, the straight-line relationship (lower left to upper right) would occur because students who scored high in one half have identically high scores in the other. The test, in this case, would have perfect reliability.

Chart B plots a scattergram distribution of rather high positive correlation which instructors are more likely to encounter with good tests. It shows that some of the students earned higher scores in one test half than in the other; but generally speaking the relationship (correlation) of the two sets of scores is fairly high. Satisfactory test reliability is suggested.

Chart C plots still another form of score distribution which sometimes occurs with tests. In this case there is an absence of relationship between the two sets of scores. Quite a number of students with high scores in one half have received lower scores on the second; another group scored just the opposite; some of the others received comparable scores in both halves. With no general discernible pattern of relationship evident for the distribution, reliability appears low. Further work seems required to lengthen the test, to choose halves of more nearly equal difficulty, to check technical difficulties with the scoring machine, or to check the consistency of scorers.

The relationship shown in Chart D is an example of perfect negative correlation. If such a relationship were to occur it would mean that students who do well in one half of the test do poorly in the other, and vice versa. This situation would not be encountered in the measurement of test reliability, and, indeed, it would be unlikely to obtain even a mild negative correlation in such cases, except as a chance variation from zero reliability. It is presented with this discussion only to round out the concept of such hypothetical relationships.

Various textbooks and manuals contain full details of other procedures for computing more accurately the reliability of one's tests. Especially recommended are the procedures employing (1) the Kuder-Richardson Formula 20, which defines reliability in terms of the internal consistency of tests, i.e., the

---

[4] Selecting test halves in this manner is considered better than taking the entire first half of the test for one score and the last half for the other. Students sometimes make better scores in the first half of a test, while they are fresh; material in one test half is often related, and if the student's preparation is such that because of this fact he does less well in one half than in the other, the correlation of scores (and, hence, reliability) will be lowered. Scores in the last half may also be similarly lowered because the student fails to answer the last few items.

degree to which each item measures the same behaviors as the test as a whole, and (2) the Pearson Produce-Moment Coefficient of Correlation.

### DEVELOPING AN ITEM FILE

It is recommended, too, that test items be typed on separate cards (5- by 8-inches is a good size) and placed in some suitable arrangement in a safely locked file for future use and revision. Each card should contain space (front and back) for stating: (1) the objective the item measures, (2) records of dates of use of the item and identification of the groups with whom it was used, (3) response tallies, (4) a discrimination index, and (5) a difficulty index. One suggested form for this purpose is given in Figure 6-3.

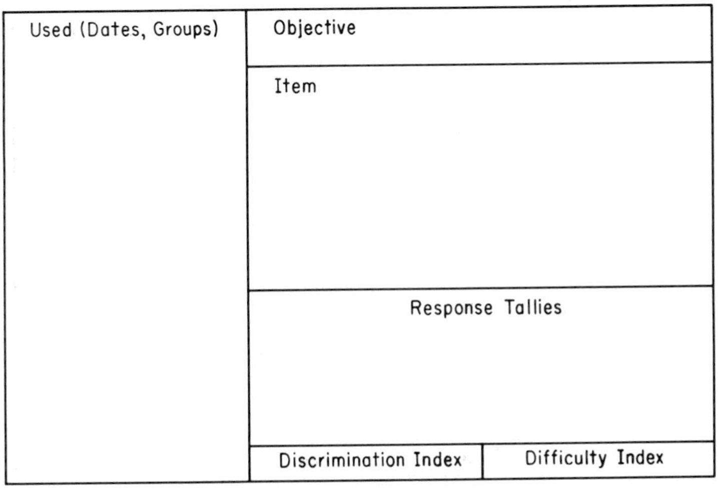

| Used (Dates, Groups) | Objective |
|---|---|
| | Item |
| | Response Tallies |
| | Discrimination Index · Difficulty Index |

**Figure 6-3.**
Suggested test item file card.

## JUDGING OTHER STUDENT WORK

College instructors are usually required to evaluate other forms of student work as well as tests. Judgments and ratings must be made of oral reports, term papers, book reports, class participation, or the performance of certain manipulative skills, to name only a few. The following questions suggest a general approach to such measurements:

What *criteria* are available or needed to rate or judge such student work? (Combined judgments of expert authorities are often used.)

What are the *major elements* of the process or product in which excellence may be demonstrated?

What are significant *subelements* of the process or product with which the total rating must be concerned?

What is the *relative importance* (or weight) of each?

What are the *bases for scaling performances or products*?

What will be the *range of scaling* (from "excellent" to "unsatisfactory," for example)? What criteria will be used to determine the range limits of each rating on the continuum? If a final, overall rating is needed, how will it be determined? Will it be the average of the weighted ratings of all elements combined? How will it be reported to students?

It is recommended that students be given advance copies of all such criterion lists to be used as aids in preparing the products or performances on which they will be judged. Use of identical lists on which to record final ratings also aids students in assessing the strengths and weaknesses of their efforts.

### JUDGING ORAL REPORTS

Evaluation of oral reports is usually concerned primarily with the facts and ideas communicated and with evidence of completeness and validity. It must obviously include some (but not major) attention to certain technical qualities of presentations. Both aspects suggest criteria such as the following:

*Sources.* Were appropriate and valid data used? Are the sources acknowledged? Did the student show evidence of having questioned the validity, representativeness, and currency of his data?

*Content and treatment.* Is the topic reported suitable to the assignment as given? Is the topic adequately covered? Are there signs of originality and creativity in the approach and treatment? Does the student personalize his data and relate it to the backgrounds and known interests of his audience? Do his facts support his conclusions? Is there evidence he has sufficiently investigated the background of the topic? Does he use language accurately?

*Structure.* Does the report have an interesting beginning and recognizable important parts or elements? Were suitable transitions made between parts? Were summaries given, as needed?

*Presentation.* Does the reporter observe time limits? Does he maintain audience contact? Does he speak easily—without hesitation, somewhat extemporaneously, without relying heavily on notes? Does he visualize or demonstrate parts of his report, as appropriate? Is he at ease before the group, in control of himself and the situation? Does he use good language? Is his use of voice effective (emphasis, volume, pacing)?

### JUDGING TERM PAPERS

A similar set of questions may be considered in evaluating student term papers:

*Sources.* Is there evidence that the writer has made a sufficiently thorough analysis of the work of others who have written on the topic? Has he evaluated the worth of such sources?

*Content and treatment.* Is there evidence of creative thinking and adaptation of ideas by the writer himself, or is his presentation largely through the thoughts of others? Does the report start somewhere and end somewhere? Is what the student has to say important and directly related to the topic—or does it relate only obliquely? Is the writer economical and pointed in his use of language? Are introductions, transitions, and summaries evident and functional? Is there acknowledgment of the use of others' ideas and findings?

*Technical.* Does the student observe format rules made for the assignment? Is the report neatly presented (typed, if required), properly spaced, and laid out? Is the use of language accurate (spelling, choice of words)?

### JUDGING BOOK REPORTS

A few additional questions may be asked in suggesting criteria by which to judge student book reports:

*Choice of books.* If books are assigned, were these the ones read? If the student chose his own, were they significant books related to the problems of the course?

*Treatment.* Does the student show the ability to synthesize ideas contained in the books, to relate them to the emphases of the course, and to generalize meaningfully? Is there evidence the student acknowledges direct or indirect use of others' ideas in his report?

*Technical.* Does the report follow the prescribed format closely enough? Is it technically well prepared (typed, if required; carefully proofread and corrected)?

### JUDGING CLASS PARTICIPATION

The contributions which students make in one's classes are sometimes used as one part of an overall evaluation for assigning course grades. In making judgments about such participation, the following criteria will apply:

*Frequency.* How often does the student contribute in class?

*Type of contribution.* Does he volunteer? Or does he only answer direct questions?

*Quality of contribution.* Are his contributions strong—suited to the occasion, well thought out? Are they founded in fact or principle, or are they simply hortatory or argumentative? Is he operating from prejudice or bias?

*Relationships in class.* Is the student sensitive to the effects of his statements on others in the class? Does he respect, or is he impatient with, other points of view? Does he facilitate intercommunication and examination of ideas within the group?

### JUDGING MANIPULATIVE SKILLS

One objective of teaching common to many areas of the college curriculum is to develop and improve various manipulative skills. Examples may be found in home economics (sewing, designing clothes), business (typing, using adding or calculating machines), engineering (using the slide rule), science (using the microscope), music (playing an instrument), and in many other fields. Evaluative criteria that apply generally in such cases include the following:

*Correctness or accuracy of performance.* Are all necessary steps of the process performed correctly and in proper sequence? If safety factors are involved, are they properly observed? Is the accuracy of performance within imposed tolerance limits?

*Speed.* Is the operation performed within expected time limits consistent with normal demands and expectations in such situations? Is precision sacrificed to speed, or vice versa?

*Understanding.* Is there evidence that the student applies appropriate principles to guide his performance? Does he understand the reasons underlying his actions? Or does he perform on a rote basis?

Performance tests that seek to measure manipulative skills should be developed as a series of tasks, beginning with the simple and ranging to the more complex. Each performance should be broken down into a series of written steps or procedures and accompanied, in each case, with qualitative rating scales to facilitate evaluation. As with all such ratings, decisions must be made concerning the relative importance, or weight, to be reflected in the evaluations.

## GRADING

The instructor's evaluation of student performance on tests and other assignments or tasks related to his courses are ordinarily translated into letter grades or numerical rankings.

### CRITICISMS OF GRADING

Recently, the entire concept of grades has been heavily criticized, if not rejected, by much of the student body and many professors in higher education. The criticism of grading follows a line of reasoning similar to the following:

> . . . We must move toward a more democratic university. To do this we must first abolish the current grading system. No step could be more central to basic reform. Grades are now the central instrument of coercion employed by the university against the students, and if students are to be allowed to participate and decide matters relating to their own academic plans, this instrument must be removed from the hands of the faculty. Grades destroy the very educational goals they purport to serve, namely, useful evaluations

of learning. By testing the student's ability to memorize facts and notes, the professor discovers only the most superficial aspects of what the student has received (or not received) from a course. By giving the student a letter grade or a percentage score, he informs the student quite inadequately about his strengths, weaknesses, and future directions. . . .

The student performs, and the professor judges, and the relationship is strictly one-way. Seldom is there any thought that the student and the teacher are somehow partners in the learning process; seldom any thought that perhaps the student might be competent to evaluate himself, *for the record*, and that such an experience in itself might be educative when done cooperatively with the professor. . . .

Getting rid of the current grading system won't be easy. Schools have been using it so long that, like a narcotic, it has become an addiction, to the point that educators are quite fearful of facing the world without grades. Often reformers go halfway, replacing grades with pass-fail, for example. While this alternative exerts less coercion on the student to compete mindlessly for a better place on the normal curve, it still leaves the student without any substantive and useful evaluation of his work, which, after all, should be the goal.

A better direction would be to encourage the student and the professor jointly to evaluate the student's work *and* the professor's contribution to that work. . . . A student ought to have a way of knowing what his skills and weaknesses are, but the grade-point average is not the most sensible way, humanely or educationally, and new ways should be developed and tried at each campus.[5]

Many institutions have responded to such arguments by offering students the choice of "pass-fail" or "credit-no credit" grades for some or all of their courses outside their major fields. A few have established a simple "pass" or "fail" as the only grades given in any course. But while reform and rethinking of the entire grading system appear to be called for, there seems to be little chance that present arrangements will be jettisoned in very many institutions within the foreseeable future. There is much more reason to believe that the grading system will be improved through expanded institutional and individual efforts of professors, students, and academic administrators who have the insight to respond to the need. Goode comments on this need:

[5] Robert S. Powell, Jr., "Participation Is Learning," *Saturday Review,* January 10, 1970, pp. 56-58.

If credits are the coinage of Academia, grades are the stamp that sets their value. ... A professor who advocates the abolition of grades, even citing successful experience in operating without them, arouses alarm; he would debase the currency. ... Faculty and students alike are aware of the unreliability of grades. Grades from one department may represent better work than the same grades from another department. A grade of A from one teacher may really equal a grade of C from another. Teachers hold very different ideas and employ very divergent systems in assigning grades. Some never fail a student, while some on the average fail one in four. Different teachers will score a paper or examination very differently. The same teacher will score the same thing differently at different times. ... As professionals, supposedly qualified not only as specialists but also as teaching operatives, we need to study our grades and grading. ... The fortuitous character of grades and grading casts professional discredit upon us. If grading were a game, we might expect and accept a large element of chance. ... Certainly the scoring of the outcomes of teaching-learning should not be a game; the issues are too grave for that.[6]

## GRADING PRACTICES

While course grades are still sometimes based exclusively on a single end-of-course examination, by far the more common practice is to report in one symbol (letter or number) the combined grades students earn in several different course activities—term papers, book reports, oral reports, discussion, quizzes, midterms, and finals.

To determine the final grade, the instructor must do three things, generally in this order: (1) assess and grade the student's performance in each of the several different activities, (2) assign suitable weights to each separate grade, and (3) combine the separate grades into a single grade in a manner that recognizes their varying weights, their variability, and the practices of the institution in which he teaches. To perform these steps fairly and accurately, the instructor is required, at the least, to make use of the elementary statistical procedures described later in this section.

Although grades and their interpretations have come to have similar meanings in most institutions, differences in standards and practices warrant their special study by beginning instructors. An excerpt from the *Faculty Handbook* of the

[6]Goode, Delmer M., "The Games of Grades," in *College and University Teaching*, ed. Herman A. Estrin and Delmer M. Goode (Dubuque, Iowa: William C. Brown Company, 1964), pp. 422-423.

Ohio State University is an example of efforts to clarify the grading process and the significance of grades in one institution:

> The grade should represent the degree of achievement in the subject matter of the course. This implies an adequate sampling of subject matter on a competitive basis by means of tests or other valid means of appraisal. The Committee (on University Grades) recognizes that evaluation of students includes aspects of development other than achievement of subject matter. The final grade in a course, however, has come to mean a measure of the ability of the student in mastering a body of organized knowledge represented by the formally organized course in which the grade is given. To assign a final grade that is an attempted synthesis of subject matter achievement, personality, attitudes, and many other factors simply destroys the meaning of such a grade since the student, the instructor, and the future employer do not know the relative weights of the various factors used in determining the grade. This point of view does not preclude the necessity for other types of evaluation. These, however, should be reported separately and may well become parts of the students' records in the various placement offices.

Most institutions seek also to describe student qualities, characteristics, or achievements associated with various letter grades, somewhat as follows:

A—Signifies that both major and minor instructional goals have been achieved and that the work is of superior quality. This grade is reserved for outstanding students who are clearly capable of going on to do advanced work in the field.

B—Major instructional goals achieved with excellent, above average, standards; some minor goals not achieved; easily capable of doing the next stage of advanced work in the field.

C—Major instructional goals achieved with minimum acceptability; many minor goals not achieved; work of average quality; minimally capable of doing advanced work in the field, with no major handicaps to performance.

D—Most major goals not achieved with even limited acceptability; below average work, but above failure.

F—No major goals achieved; work of unacceptable quality.

## THE NORMAL-CURVE CONCEPT

The normal curve, as illustrated in Figure 6-4, plots the usual distribution of random samples of natural phenomena, such as inches of height in adult males,

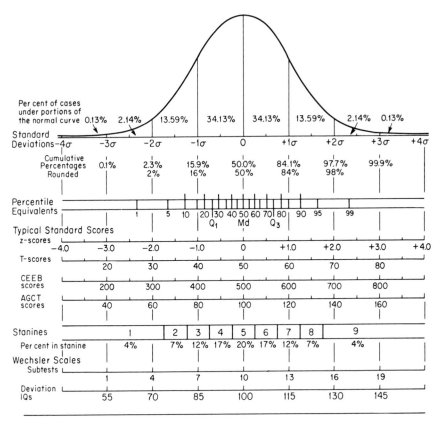

**Figure 6-4.**
Normal curve adaptations. Source: "Methods of Expressing Test Scores," *Test Service Bulletin* 48(1955):2. The Psychological Corporation, 522 Fifth Avenue, New York.

scores of unselected fifteen-year-old girls in aptitude tests, or feet of snow on Pike's Peak over the period of the last fifty years. Figures in such distributions tend to be plotted symmetrically about the mean, with concentrations at the middle and a thinning out toward the extremes.

Use of the normal curve as a rigid framework for the assignment of college grades has been criticized. Faculty members of the Ohio State University, for example, are told in their official handbook:

The use of the normal curve of probability should not be applied as a means of arriving at grades, particularly for relatively small sections. The normal curve is in reality an assumption. While the distribution of any one of a number of characteristics of a large group of individuals follows roughly the normal curve, no distribution has ever been found which follows the so-called normal curve. Furthermore, the distribution tends to vary from the normal curve to the degree that selective factors are operating. College students are in many ways a select group of the total population and logically are less likely to follow the normal curve, particularly with respect to those characteristics involving the possession and application of academic intelligence. The grades for students in required classes are likely to present a different pattern of distribution from that for students in elective courses. This is usually true with respect to grade patterns for different course levels. The Committee (on University Grades) recognizes that the array of grades for any course or the marks for any examination will usually show some distribution. This distribution, however, should not be forced into a fixed pattern as is done when the normal curve is used.

Dressel and Nelson cite similar arguments against rigid application of the normal-curve concept to the grading of college work. They are especially critical of inflexible uses of the curve in determining fixed or standard percentages of A's, B's, C's, D's, and F's:[7]

> Only by making certain assumptions is it possible to assign such percentages. When these assumptions regarding the number of standard units in the range of distribution and the equality in standard unit of each of the grade ranges are stripped of their mathematical cloaks of obscurity, it becomes clear that the entire process is a matter of preference. That being the case, it is more realistic to decide on the percentage directly than to adopt some distribution based upon unjustified premises.

What, then, should be the recommended limits for the percentages of grades in various categories? How many A's, B's, C's, D's, and F's should be given? Obviously, any answer to these questions should take into account the fact that the grade distribution pattern must reflect general standards of the department and of the institution as a whole as well as those of the instructor himself. Excessively high percentages of A's or F's are usually difficult to justify. The system selected must also be adapted to the conditions under which it is used. It

---

[7]Paul L. Dressel and Clarence H. Nelson, "Testing and Grading Policies," in *Evaluation in Higher Education,* ed. Paul L. Dressel (Boston: Houghton Mifflin Company, 1961), p. 230.

is possible that any predetermined percentage system (even one with consider-able flexibility built into it) will be inappropriate for use with some students. A group of highly selected honor students, for example, almost certainly would be expected to earn an abnormal proportion of A's or B's.

Dressel and Nelson report that in several multisection courses at Michigan State University, the recommended pattern of grading in use for some time has been A, 0 to 15 percent; B, 20 to 30 percent; C, 40 to 50 percent; D, 10 to 20 percent; and F, 0 to 1 percent. They note that such ranges permit grading flexibility and that the assignment of more A's and B's than D's and F's may be expected.[8]

## ASSIGNING GRADES TO SCORES

One recommended means of assigning grades to test scores or to scores assigned to other course activities is based on the following procedures:

Prepare a *frequency distribution* of the scores (obtained, in this case, from use of a four-response multiple-choice test of 100 items). Tally each score in its proper place on the list. Unless the number of cases is large or the range of scores extended, interval distributions are not needed.

As part of the further process of using this distribution in assigning grades, several questions should be asked (note that figures and comments below refer to the distribution of scores in Table 1):

What is the *range of scores*? (61 to 92, or 32 points, in this case.)

What is the *median score*—the score in the middle position, above which 50 percent of the scores fall? (In this case it is the score of 79, obtained by counting up from the bottom through half the total number of scores in the distribution.)

Is the range sufficiently large to suggest satisfactory *discrimination of ability* within the group measured? (It appears to be.)

How does the highest score compare with the *maximum possible score* for the test? Is there evidence that the test discriminated at the top of the ability range of the class? (Yes.)

[8]*Ibid.*, p. 230.

**TABLE 1.**
Sample score and grade computation for a four-alternative
multiple-choice examination of 100 items

| Raw test score (of 100) | Tallies | Frequency | Grade | % (approx.) |
|---|---|---|---|---|
| 92 | 1 | 1 | A | 11 |
| 91 | 1 | 1 | A | |
| 90 | 1 | 1 | A | |
| 89 | 11 | 2 | A− | |
| 88 | | | | |
| 87 | 11 | 2 | B+ | |
| 86 | 11 | 2 | B | |
| 85 | 111 | 3 | B | 21 |
| 84 | 11 | 2 | B− | |
| 83 | | | | |
| 82 | | | | |
| 81 | 111 | 3 | C+ | |
| 80 | 1111 | 4 | C+ | |
| 79 median | 1 median | 1 | C | |
| 78 | 111 | 3 | C | |
| 77 | | | | |
| 76 | 111 | 3 | C | |
| 75 | 11 | 2 | C | 53 |
| 74 | 11 | 2 | C− | |
| 73 | 1 | 1 | C− | |
| 72 | 11 | 2 | C− | |
| 71 | 11 | 2 | C− | |
| 70 | | | | |
| 69 | | | | |
| 68 | | | | |
| 67 | | | | |
| 66 | 11 | 2 | D | |
| 65 | | | | 10 |
| 64 | 11 | 2 | D | |
| 63 | | | | |
| 62 | 1 | 1 | F | |
| 61 | 1 | 1 | F | 5 |
| | 43 | 43 | | 100 |

How does the lowest score compare with a *chance score* for this type of test? (Satisfactorily above it.)

Are the scores quite *well distributed* within the range? (Yes, with concentrations in the middle range, as would be expected.)

Do *concentrations and breaks* occur within the distribution pattern and suggest logical limits for various grade categories? Do scores earned appear to justify award of A's and F's? (They appear to.)

Does it appear *possible to assign grades* within the pattern limits usually adhered to within the institution, taking into account the nature of the student group involved? (Probably.)

Mowry and Berg recommend another procedure for assigning grades which employs an average deviation technique. They indicate that it has the advantage of taking into account the magnitude rather than simply the rank order of each score. Grades are determined on the basis of how far scores deviate from the average score earned in the test. The steps in converting scores to letter grades, with this procedure, are as follows:

1. List the raw scores in a column in ascending or descending order.
2. Find the average of these scores to the nearest whole number.
3. Opposite each raw score give the difference between it and the average score (these are the deviations of each score from the average).
4. Add these deviations[9] and find their average to one decimal point (this figure is the "average deviation").
5. Assign grade limits on the following basis:
   a. Two times the average deviation plus the average is the lower limit of the A's.
   b. Two thirds of the average deviation plus the average is the lower limit of the B's.
   c. Two thirds of the average deviation subtracted from the average is the lower limit of the C's.
   d. Two times the average deviation subtracted from the average is the lower limit of the D's.

This procedure will ordinarily yield about 5 percent A's, 25 percent B's, 40

[9]Ignoring the positive or negative signs; otherwise the addition of all deviations would result in zero.

percent C's, 25 percent D's, and 5 percent F's, although justifiable variations must often be made due to the special characteristics of the group measured.[10]

## COMBINING GRADES FOR FINAL GRADES

To arrive at final grades in a course, the instructor must usually bring together and average the grades students have earned in a number of course activities. The problem is one of deciding how to weight these grades so as to recognize the importance and variability of each in relation to a final grade.

One feasible means of doing this, when distributed letter grades have been assigned (as suggested in the materials first discussed), is to convert each letter grade into points in accordance with some factor related to its importance. Suppose, for example, that a student earned grades, as follows:

### TABLE 2.

| Activity | Grade and grade points* | Weight factor | Score points |
|---|---|---|---|
| 1. first midterm examination | B (3) | 1 | 3 |
| 2. second midterm examination | C (2) | 1 | 2 |
| 3. class participation | B (3) | 1 | 3 |
| 4. term paper | A (4) | 2 | 8 |
| 5. book report | A (4) | ½ | 2 |
| 6. book report | A (4) | ½ | 2 |
| 7. final examination | B (3) | 2 | 6 |
| Total | | 8 | 26 |

*If plus or minus signs were used in such computations, this further differentiation of weight could be recognized by increasing points for grades and using another value scale, as follows: A+, 14; A, 13; A−, 12; B+, 11; B, 10; B−, 9; C+, 8; C, 7; C−, 6; D+, 5; D, 4; D−, 3; F+, 2; F, 1; F−, 0.

In this example, A is valued at 4 points, B at 3, C at 2, D at 1, and F at 0.[11] The "factor" refers to the weight value of each grade. The term paper, in this

[10]George E. Mowry and Harry D. Berg, *Instructor's Manual to Accompany A Short History of American Democracy* (by John D. Hicks and George E. Mowry), (Boston: Houghton Mifflin Company, 1956), pp. vii-viii.

[11]The range of weight to this grading scheme is typically as follows: A, 3.5 to 4.0; B, 2.5 to 3.5; C, 1.5 to 2.5, D, 0.5 to 1.5; and F, 0 to 0.5.

case, is weighted twice as heavily as a midterm examination, while a book report has only half its weight.

One procedure for assigning grades from such computations is to determine the *average score points* earned (26/8 or 3.25, or a B, in the case shown) or to translate total points into letter grades without the division operation. A second procedure would be to make a new distribution of the total points as computed for each student's course activities and to assign new grades on the basis of positions of students in that distribution in the same manner as test grades were computed earlier in this chapter. Instructors will recognize, of course, that under this plan students who earned low A's or other "minus" grades in various activities throughout the term could conceivably be moved into different categories if the end-of-course totals are redistributed and then regraded. Students should ordinarily be informed of any such plan early in the semester. Grades assigned for various course requirements completed during the term should then be regarded only as a tentative indication of the level of a student's performance, subject to later evaluation in the final distribution of grades.

Other more detailed and refined procedures for preparing distributions of final grades, discussed in various standard sources, include percentile ranks, z scores, and $T$ scores.

## MEASURING INTERESTS AND ATTITUDES

The college instructor sometimes wishes to learn something about the interests and attitudes of his students and to estimate the extent to which discerned changes may be attributed to instruction. These subjective measurements are helpful additional data with which to assess the progress of students toward important instructional goals. In most cases, these data should be collected anonymously, and students should be informed that results have no bearing on grades for the course. The reason for this is primarily that students will, occasionally, make responses they assume to be desired by the instructor.

Data with which to make judgments about student attitudes and interests may come from a variety of sources:

From the "feel" of the class, which often comes somewhat intuitively with increased experience in teaching

From direct observation and questioning of students—as during personal interviews

From standardized interest inventories or attitude scales (e.g., the Kuder Preference Record, Strong Vocational Interest Blank, and others)

From analyses of instructor-made interest inventories, opinionnaires, or attitude scales

Principal attention will be given here to the latter type—the instructor-made devices for measuring interests and attitudes.

College instructors find that information about aspects of their courses which seem to hold greatest interest for their students is useful. It can involve students in planning the course by helping to select topics or activities of high interest to

**TABLE 3.**
**Interest questionnaire form**

DIRECTIONS: Following are a number of possible topics and activities for this course, some of which may be of more interest to you than others. There will not be time during the course to devote attention to all of them; some choices must be made as to which to include and which to omit or to present through outside assignments and activities. To assist in these choices, please check the appropriate rating to indicate the degree of your interest in each item in the following list:

| Degree of interest | | | | No. | Item |
|---|---|---|---|---|---|
| High | Average | Low | No basis for judging | | |
| | | | | | |

## TABLE 4.
### Opinionnaire form

DIRECTIONS: Following is a series of generalizations, principles, or ideas expected to be considered in this course. You may or may not agree with them; or you may support some more strongly than others. Please circle the rating for each item which seems to be the one representing most closely your point of view or belief with respect to it. In making your rating, use the following symbols:

SA—strongly agree with the statement
A—agree with the statement
U—uncertain; have no opinion either way
D—disagree with the statement
SD—strongly disagree with the statement

| Your rating | | | | | No. | Item |
|---|---|---|---|---|---|---|
| SA | A | U | D | SD | 1 | |
| SA | A | U | D | SD | 2 | |

them. Even when there is no possibility of choice, it provides clues about topics or activities to which the instructor may give special attention in stressing their significance or value in the course.

One means of obtaining data with which to assess student interest in a course is to prepare a list of potential topics and activities and ask students to rate their interest in each—"high," "average," "low," or "no basis for judging," as indicated in Table 3.

This list might also be used (with perhaps a differently structured introductory statement) as a basis for comparing earlier interest ratings with end-of-course ratings on the same topics and activities.

It is possible to obtain similar data for tentative judgments of student attitudes one hopes to develop through his courses. A rating sheet such as that in Table 4, given early in the course and again toward the end, offers a means of comparing changes occurring in the interval.

Interpretations of scaled instruments of the types discussed above may range from simple to complex, but perhaps the most common practices are represented in the following suggestions:

Make a simple tally of responses to each choice with each item.

Determine which ratings stand out from others in the list.

Study differences and similarities of ratings for types of individuals in the rating group; major versus nonmajors, men versus women, capable versus average or below-average students. Seek explanations of observed differences through consideration of other known data about these groups.

Consider the significance of these differences insofar as the planning and teaching of the course are concerned.

## EVALUATING THE INSTRUCTOR

The college instructor who wishes to learn more about his overall effectiveness as a teacher has access to several sources of information. He may (1) analyze his teaching practices by introspection, (2) study the educational product, (3) "mirror" his teaching practices through colleagues, student committees, or audio- or videotape recordings, or (4) go directly to students to ask their opinions.[12]

### INTROSPECTIVE ANALYSES

Introspective analyses of one's teaching practices are useful whether or not other evaluative activities are undertaken. The instructor may ask: Am I satisfied with results of my teaching? Have I managed to maintain the enthusiasm it needs? Am I in a rut? Have I defined and stated my course objectives clearly? Do my presentations and assignments clearly relate to these objectives? Am I as fully prepared for the class as I should be? Am I up-to-date on new developments in the field?

### STUDY OF THE EDUCATIONAL PRODUCT

Studying the educational product involves efforts to appraise changes brought about in students which may be attributed to the educational activities of the

[12]Materials in this section are adapted chiefly from the author's contributions to "Evaluating College Teaching," in *Curriculum Reporter Supplement* No. 1, ed. John Banister (San Jose, California: San Jose State College, 1965).

class, as discussed in this chapter. As has been pointed out, particularly helpful sources of data for this purpose are one's tests. The answers students give to one's questions provide numerous insights into their thinking, their study habits, their grasp of course essentials, or their special strengths or deficiencies. Such insights also provide the instructor with cues for ameliorative action or changes in ways of conducting the course.

Anyone analyzing the educational product must recognize that much of what students know, appreciate, or are able to do cannot be attributed only to the work they do in his classes. Aptitude, previous experience and achievement, and current activities in other classes, or entirely outside of class, must also be considered. Pretesting, therefore, is a valuable means of identifying beginning levels of accomplishment and of providing benchmarks against which to compare end-of-semester achievement.

### MIRRORING

Mirroring one's teaching is accomplished in several ways—the simplest is to ask a colleague to sit in on one's class and to frankly appraise the strengths and weaknesses he observes. However, friendships may be stretched, if not broken, by making negative statements vis-à-vis. This problem may be overcome, in part, by appointing a small committee of students from the class to give particular attention, as the course proceeds, to students' points of view about the way things are going. An occasional meeting of the instructor and the committee may provide essential feedback and suggest needed changes of procedure or emphasis.

The audio- or videotape recording of one or more class sessions is also a means of mirroring instructor-student or student-student relationships in the classroom as bases for judging the effectiveness of classroom teaching procedures. The taped content of a class session may reveal (1) the extent of student participation—the number and frequency of student responses, the number of different students who participate, (2) the quality of student comments and the questions asked, (3) the incidence of student restlessness or hostility, as revealed in comments, shufflings, tones of voice, (4) the types of instructor contributions to the class period—lecture only, leading discussion, explanations and elaborations, challenges to thought, summaries, (5) the quality and quantity of instructor contributions (Did he dominate unnecessarily? Were the contributions of high quality?), and (6) distracting instructor mannerisms which should be corrected.

## STUDENT OPINION

Despite strong opinions by some instructors that there is little of value to come from student judgments of teaching effectiveness, greater attention is now being given these evaluative data in institutions all over the country. A survey by Stecklein, for example, indicated that of 800 reporting colleges, nearly 40 percent used student ratings regularly and another 32 percent have considered using them.[13]

Riley and associates concluded that ratings given college teachers by their students were consistent with those made by trained, experienced observers, and that the quality of work done by a student in a course did not affect significantly his subsequent rating of the instructor.[14] Guthrie, whose pioneer work reflected the most extensive research in faculty ratings by students, argued that student evaluations, when carefully and properly handled, provided the best criterion of quality of instruction.[15]

Although many different kinds of opinionnaires are used, their similarities of purpose are clear. These instruments usually provide opportunities for students to react to such varied facets of instruction as (1) course objectives, (2) organization and management of course activities, (3) the instructor himself—his qualifications in the subject, his general educational background, or his personal characteristics (including mannerisms, voice, "approachability," concern with student problems, sense of humor, and enthusiasm), (4) instructional techniques and procedures used in the class, (5) assignments, and (6) examinations and other evaluation of student performance.

These matters are sometimes studied from answers students give to open-ended statements such as "My interest in this class . . . ," "The text we have used this semester . . . ," or "I would recommend that this course . . . ." Another method of study used by one instructor[16] involved distribution at the last regular meeting of the class of a single sheet of paper, at the top of which appeared the following statement: "In the large, inviting space below, type or print your opinions of textbooks, methods, content, and teacher of this course.

[13] John E. Stecklein, "Colleges and Universities—Programs," *Encyclopedia of Educational Research* (New York: The Macmillan Company, 1960), p. 287.

[14] John W. Riley, Bruce F. Ryan, and Marcia Lifshitz, *The Student Looks at His Teacher,* (New Brunswick, N. J.: Rutgers University Press, 1950).

[15] E. R. Guthrie, *The Evaluation of Teaching: A Progress Report* (Seattle: University of Washington, 1954).

[16] Dr. Lew Girdler, Department of English, San Jose State College.

Suggestions toward improvement will be especially welcome. Sign your name if you like; but I would prefer that you do not. These sheets will be collected at the final examination, but I shall not read them until after I have turned in semester grades."

But probably the most common means of collecting student opinions of college teaching is the structured opinionnaire, such as that developed and used at San Jose State College.

### San Jose State College

### INSTRUCTOR RATING SCALE

### DO NOT SIGN YOUR NAME, BUT PLEASE
### RATE EACH ITEM HONESTLY

**DIRECTIONS TO STUDENTS:** In order to secure information which may lead to the improvement of instruction in this college, you are asked to rate your instructor on EACH of the items listed. On each line make an (X) at the place which seems to you most appropriate for the instructor you are rating. The highest possible rating for an item is 10, the lowest is 0, with nine gradations between. To aid you in making your marking, note the three descriptions for each item, one at the left for the best rating, one at the right for the poorest rating, and one in the middle for the average rating.

**1. OBJECTIVES CLARIFIED BY INSTRUCTOR**

| 10 | 9 | 8 | 7 | 6 | 5 | 4 | 3 | 2 | 1 | 0 |
|---|---|---|---|---|---|---|---|---|---|---|

| Objectives clearly defined. | Objectives somewhat vague or indefinite | Objectives very vague or given no attention. |
|---|---|---|

**2. ORGANIZATION OF COURSE**

| 10 | 9 | 8 | 7 | 6 | 5 | 4 | 3 | 2 | 1 | 0 |
|---|---|---|---|---|---|---|---|---|---|---|

| Course exceptionally well organized; subject matter in agreement with course objectives. | Course satisfactorily organized; subject matter fairly well suited to objectives. | Organization very poor; subject matter frequently unrelated to objectives. |
|---|---|---|

**3. KNOWLEDGE OF SUBJECT**

| 10 | 9 | 8 | 7 | 6 | 5 | 4 | 3 | 2 | 1 | 0 |
|---|---|---|---|---|---|---|---|---|---|---|

| Knowledge of subject broad, accurate, up-to-date. | Knowledge of subject somewhat limited and at times not up-to-date. | Knowledge of subject seriously deficient and frequently inaccurate and out-of-date. |
|---|---|---|

**4. RANGE OF INTERESTS AND CULTURE**

| 10 | 9 | 8 | 7 | 6 | 5 | 4 | 3 | 2 | 1 | 0 |
|---|---|---|---|---|---|---|---|---|---|---|
| Instructor has very broad interests and culture; frequently relates course to other fields and to present-day problems. | | | Instructor has fair breadth of interests and culture; occasionally relates subject to other fields and to present-day problems. | | | | Instructor is narrow in his interests and culture; seldom relates subject to other fields or to present-day problems. | | | |

**5. VARIETY IN CLASSROOM TECHNIQUES**

| 10 | 9 | 8 | 7 | 6 | 5 | 4 | 3 | 2 | 1 | 0 |
|---|---|---|---|---|---|---|---|---|---|---|
| Effective and varied use of classroom methods and techniques: lecture, discussion, demonstration, visual aids. | | | Occasionally changes method from straight lecture or discussion. | | | | Uses one method almost exclusively; all class hours seem alike. | | | |

**6. ASSIGNMENTS**

| 10 | 9 | 8 | 7 | 6 | 5 | 4 | 3 | 2 | 1 | 0 |
|---|---|---|---|---|---|---|---|---|---|---|
| Clear, reasonable, coordinated with class work. | | | Occasionally indefinite and unrealted to class work. | | | | Confused, often made late, with no relation to work of course. | | | |

**7. ABILITY TO AROUSE INTEREST**

| 10 | 9 | 8 | 7 | 6 | 5 | 4 | 3 | 2 | 1 | 0 |
|---|---|---|---|---|---|---|---|---|---|---|
| Interest among students usually runs high | | | Students seem only mildly interested. | | | | Majority of students inattentive most of the time. | | | |

**8. SKILL IN GUIDING THE LEARNING PROCESS**

| 10 | 9 | 8 | 7 | 6 | 5 | 4 | 3 | 2 | 1 | 0 |
|---|---|---|---|---|---|---|---|---|---|---|
| Gives student opportunity to think and learn independently, critically, and creatively. | | | Gives student some opportunity to develop his academic resources on his own initiative. | | | | Little or no attention to student ideas; ignores or discourages original and independent effort. | | | |

**9. MANNERISMS**

| 10 | 9 | 8 | 7 | 6 | 5 | 4 | 3 | 2 | 1 | 0 |
|---|---|---|---|---|---|---|---|---|---|---|
| Manner pleasing; free from annoying mannerisms. | | | Mannerisms not seriously objectionable. | | | | Constantly exhibits annoying mannerisms. | | | |

**10. FAIRNESS IN GRADING**

| 10 | 9 | 8 | 7 | 6 | 5 | 4 | 3 | 2 | 1 | 0 |
|---|---|---|---|---|---|---|---|---|---|---|
| Fair and impartial; grades based on several evidences of achievement. | | | Partial at times; grades based on a few evidences of achievement. | | | | Frequently shows partiality; grades based on very limited evidences of achievement. | | | |

**11. WILLINGNESS TO HELP**

| 10 | 9 | 8 | 7 | 6 | 5 | 4 | 3 | 2 | 1 | 0 |
|---|---|---|---|---|---|---|---|---|---|---|

| | | |
|---|---|---|
| Instructor exceptionally friendly; usually willing to help students even if busy. | Instructor moderately friendly; usually willing to help students. | Instructor aloof or sarcastic and preoccupied; unwilling to help students. |

**12. PERSONAL ATTENTION TO STUDENT PRODUCT**

| 10 | 9 | 8 | 7 | 6 | 5 | 4 | 3 | 2 | 1 | 0 |
|---|---|---|---|---|---|---|---|---|---|---|

| | | |
|---|---|---|
| Gives close personal attention to and recognition of student's product: examination, term paper, theme, notebook. | Reads his own papers but does not comment very generously or helpfully. | Invariably pushes reading and judgments off onto reader or assistant; reads student's work superficially. |

**13. RECOGNITION OF OWN LIMITATIONS**

| 10 | 9 | 8 | 7 | 6 | 5 | 4 | 3 | 2 | 1 | 0 |
|---|---|---|---|---|---|---|---|---|---|---|

| | | |
|---|---|---|
| Welcomes differences of opinion; honest in admitting when he does not know. | Moderately tolerant of different viewpoints; usually willing to admit when he does not know. | Displeased by opposite viewpoints; dogmatic and argumentative even when clearly wrong. |

**14. SPEECH AND ENUNCIATION**

| 10 | 9 | 8 | 7 | 6 | 5 | 4 | 3 | 2 | 1 | 0 |
|---|---|---|---|---|---|---|---|---|---|---|

| | | |
|---|---|---|
| Speaks clearly and distinctly. | Words sometimes indistinct and hard to hear. | Words very indistinct; often impossible to hear. |

**15. SENSE OF HUMOR**

| 10 | 9 | 8 | 7 | 6 | 5 | 4 | 3 | 2 | 1 | 0 |
|---|---|---|---|---|---|---|---|---|---|---|

| | | |
|---|---|---|
| Enjoys a good joke (even when it is on himself); yet knows when to be serious. | Unpredictable; sometimes pleasant and happy; at other times downcast. | Poor sport; never sees the humorous side of any situation. |

**16. GENERAL ESTIMATE OF TEACHER**

| 10 | 9 | 8 | 7 | 6 | 5 | 4 | 3 | 2 | 1 | 0 |
|---|---|---|---|---|---|---|---|---|---|---|

| | | |
|---|---|---|
| Very superior teacher. | Average teacher. | Very poor teacher. |

**17. GENERAL ESTIMATE OF THE COURSE**

| 10 | 9 | 8 | 7 | 6 | 5 | 4 | 3 | 2 | 1 | 0 |
|---|---|---|---|---|---|---|---|---|---|---|

| | | |
|---|---|---|
| One of the most interesting, informative, useful, personally helpful courses. | About average in interest, usefulness, etc. | One of the least interesting, informative, useful, personally helpful courses. |

**18. ADDITIONAL COMMENTS:**

With all such rating forms, the instructor must exercise considerable caution and restraint. Attention should be given more to the *pattern* of student responses, item by item, than to either totals or averages. Patterns may be determined first by tallying the distribution of ratings for the various items and then by examining results to isolate ratings which stand out as different from the others. Special attention may be given later to these items during conferences with individual students or, occasionally, in a class discussion.

## EVALUATING LECTURING TECHNIQUES

Several alternative opportunities are open to instructors wishing to evaluate their effectiveness as lecturers. For example, they may:

Make an audio- or videotape recording of an entire lecture. While this is for some an unnerving experience, it does provide opportunities for later, detached analysis of one's techniques. Save an early tape recording to compare with one made at some later date following efforts to improve.

Invite a colleague to sit in on the lecture to give his evaluations.

Invite students to submit evaluations of lectures and suggestions for improving them. Such suggestions may come from a student committee of the class given this assignment in advance. Evaluations may sometimes be sought in private office interviews.

Check on student note-taking skills as well as their own lecturing effectiveness by requiring students to bring their notes to office interviews. A quick reading is sometimes sufficient to reveal reasons for student difficulties in the course (insufficient information, poorly organized notes, inaccurate information), some of which may be attributed to instructor performance.

Give quizzes in class immediately following presentations of points in a lecture, and assess accuracy or insight of responses.

Analyze examinations to determine the extent to which misconceptions or lack of communication may have resulted from lectures.

## SUMMARY

This chapter has developed the point of view that, through various evaluative activities, instructors and students are helped to learn more about their effectiveness as teachers and learners. Attention was given first to the purposes of evaluation and to the steps through which it is accomplished. A major emphasis was put on the analysis of various test forms used most frequently in college teaching; the so-called subjective essay tests and several objective types represented by true-false, multiple-choice, matching, and completion and short-answer items. Criteria were considered for developing, administering, and refining and improving all of these items.

Means of evaluating other types of student work were also introduced: various rating scales for judging oral reports, term papers, book reports, class participation, or manipulative skills.

A discussion of the implications and significance of grades, and means of computing and reporting them, was followed by a brief description of classroom uses of scales for assessing student interests and attitudes. A final section of the chapter described ways in which student judgments of instructor effectiveness may be used to improve teaching.

Lehmann's comments highlight the importance and role of all of these activities in evaluating college teaching:[17]

> Study and experimentation with various instructional procedures are essential. Experimentation focuses attention on teaching and learning; it can lead to procedures which are at once better and more economical. The prime characteristic of the good teacher is that he continually seeks to find in his students the effects of his teaching, and he continually modifies his teaching in response to his findings . . . he should be assisted in this task and rewarded for it.

## RELATED READING

Anastasi, Anne. *Testing Problems in Perspective.* Washington: American Council on Education, 1966.

Dressel, Paul L., et al. *Evaluation in Higher Education.* Boston: Houghton Mifflin Company, 1961.

Gronlund, Norman E., *Constructing Achievement Tests.* Englewood Cliffs, N. J.: Prentice-Hall, Inc., 1968.

[17]Irvin J. Lehmann, "Evaluation of Instruction," in *Evaluation in Higher Education*, ed. Paul L. Dressel (New York: Harper & Row, Publishers, Inc., 1961), pp. 357-358.

Jacobs, Paul I., et al. *A Guide to Evaluating Self-Instructional Programs.* New York: Holt, Rinehart and Winston, 1966..

Marshall, Max S. *Teaching Without Grades.* Corvallis, Oregon: Oregon State University Press, 1968.

Montgomery, Robert J. *Examinations.* Pittsburgh: University of Pittsburgh Press, 1968.

Nedelsky, Leo. *Science Teaching and Testing.* New York: Harcourt, Brace and World, 1965.

Richards, James M., Jr., et al. *The Assessment of Student Accomplishment in College.* Ames, Iowa: American College Testing Program, 1966.

Wilhelms, Fred T. (ed.). *Evaluation as Feedback and Guide.* Washington: Association for Supervision and Curriculum Development, 1967.

Wood, Dorothy Adkins. *Test Construction: Development and Interpretation of Achievement Tests.* Columbus, Ohio: Charles E. Merrill Books, Inc., 1961.

# index